foreword

At Orchids – The International School, we believe in providing quality education to our students through imbibing Indian values and adopting international methods. Quality education is not only about a child's all round growth and development but is also essentially discovering hidden talents and skills of children and honing these by guiding their learning, to achieve success and fulfillment in life.

We plan to achieve this goal for every child through state-of-the-art indoor and outdoor infrastructure, child-centric focus, best-in-class teachers to student's ratio and an integrated curriculum. In this endeavour, the role of parents, for us at Orchids, is a pivotal one.

In today's modern progressive world, parenting has become a demanding and challenging task for each and every one of you. At Orchids, it is our sincere endeavour to make education a learning experience not only for our children but also for their parents. Whilst a teacher or a tutor can only open a child's mind to education, it is our strong belief and conviction that parenting is what makes the difference.

In keeping with our goals and vision to move hand-in-hand with the parent body, we invite you to be a part of the success story of your children and introduce you to 'ABCs OF PARENTING' authored by writer and counselor Gouri Dange.

With our out-of-the-box and innovative thinking, and with your parenting skills, the sky is the limit for your children.

ABCs OF PARENTING

A PARENTING PRIMER

GOURI DANGE

JAICO PUBLISHING HOUSE

Ahmedabad Bangalore Bhopal Bhubaneswar Chennai
Delhi Hyderabad Kolkata Lucknow Mumbai

Published by Jaico Publishing House
A-2 Jash Chambers, 7-A Sir Phirozshah Mehta Road
Fort, Mumbai - 400 001
jaicopub@jaicobooks.com
www.jaicobooks.com

ABCs OF PARENTING
ISBN 978-81-7992-820-2

Jaico Impression: 2013

Printed by
Repro India Limited
Plot No. 50/2, T.T.C. MIDC Industrial Area
Mahape, Navi Mumbai - 400 710

acknowledgements

I would like to thank journalist and editor Pradyuman Maheshwari for first offering me the space to bring together my counseling and writing skills. Dr Dayal Mirchandani and Drs Rajan and Minnu Bhonsle who taught me how to watch and listen to families and their dynamics, without intruding or judging. Dr Ashok Ranade nudged and prodded me to bring out this book. I am also indebted to Priya Ramani and Sumana Mukherjee of Mint-Lounge and the readers of that paper. My publishers, Jaico Publishing House, have been a pleasure to work with. Always courteous, punctual and uncomplicated! Thank you.

Introduction

There are no schools for parenting; there is no apprenticeship or training period either. Most of us are simply thrown in at the deep end and are expected not just to float, but to swim strong and straight and enjoy it too!

ABCs of Parenting is a primer for those contemplating parenthood as well as for those in the thick of parenting, as also for those who are 'para-parents' – grandparents, aunts, uncles, close family friends, and teachers who interact closely with children.

Just as there are no schools for parents, there are so many key life issues that children are simply not taught, tested, corrected or rewarded for in school. These lessons are best learnt in the family – at the dining table, before bed, during playtime, in the kitchen, during a family crisis. These are rich moments in which our children acquire and sharpen their emotional intelligence. ABCs of Parenting provides key insights and tips on a wide range of topics – there's literally something for every letter of the alphabet.

Contents

acknowledgements ... iii

introduction ... v

1. a for Apologies ... 1
2. b for Boundaries ... 4
3. b for Bullying ... 7
4. c for Comparisons ... 10
5. c for Counsellor ... 13
6. c for Criticism ... 16
7. d for Discipline ... 19
8. e for Emotional Intelligence ... 22
9. e for Excelling ... 25
10. e for Expectations ... 28
11. f for Farewells ... 31
12. g for Godparents ... 34
13. g for Grandparents ... 38
14. g for Guilt ... 41
15. h for Harmony ... 44
16. i for Imagination ... 47
17. i for Interrupting ... 50

18. j for Jealousy   ...   53
19. k for Kindness   ...   56
20. l for Letting Be   ...   59
21. l for Lying   ...   62
22. m for Mealtimes   ...   65
23. m for Money   ...   68
24. n for No   ...   71
25. o for Only Child   ...   75
26. p for Personality   ...   78
27. p for Pets   ...   81
28. p for Privacy   ...   84
29. p for Punishment   ...   87
30. r for Results   ...   90
31. s for Self-Esteem   ...   93
32. s for Sex Education   ...   96
33. s for Social Skills   ...   99
34. t for Thank You   ...   102
35. u for Updating   ...   105
36. v for Violence   ...   108
37. w for Waistlines   ...   111
38. w for Winning   ...   115
39. y for Yelling   ...   118
40. z for Zombies   ...   121

a for apologies

Learning to apologize as well as to forgive, is an important life skill.

So many of us have yet not acquired the simple skill of saying we're sorry, even in adulthood. Contrary to what some people think, and most children at first believe, apologizing is not a sign of weakness or a sign that you are a bad person. It is, in fact, a sign of strength. It is a demonstration that you have the moral fibre to identify your own mistake, and the courage to express this to whoever you have wronged or hurt.

Teaching a child to say sorry involves a complex set of responses on the part of a parent. It involves teaching your child to be empathetic: Which means, learning to put himself in the shoes of the person who he has hurt. Few kids before the age of five are able to imagine how someone else feels. This emotional skill has to be fostered by the parent.

Helping a child learn to admit when a mistake or inappropriate action occurs is an important part of developing a child's character, and preparing children to relate to others. How do we teach this rather abstract, but essential social skill?

👁 Like most other skills, one teaches by example. When your kids see adults within the family offering a genuine apology, or making amends for a mistake or error, this goes a long way. Also, saying sorry to your child for forgetting to do something for him, or for wrongly mistrusting her, or for losing your temper in a completely uncalled for way…makes both you and your child better people.

👁 When your child does something hurtful to someone else or to you, spell out that you are hurt, rather than angry. If you merely show anger, your child is bound to be afraid to apologize, for fear of being stamped 'guilty', and may feel obliged to steadfastly refuse to accept his mistake, leave alone apologize.

👁 Once you have shown that your child's action has hurt you, and that an apology is called for, let your child 'feel the heat' of your reaction. Demonstrate that you are hurt and that there is something that he can do to change the situation. Do not demand an apology; rather, create an atmosphere where apologizing becomes the most genuine, natural and appropriate thing for him to do.

👁 With older children, once your child does apologize, show sincere appreciation, but don't rush to suddenly change the mood, the minute sorry has been said. Remain with the sobering mood for a while. This does not mean that you remain hurt and upset and unforgiving. It only means that you avoid teaching your children to merely use the word sorry glibly, like some magic button, so that they learn the true nature of a genuine apology.

⊛ Be careful not to rob your child of her pride and dignity, when you insist that she apologizes to you or to someone else. There is no point in making a scene or a public spectacle out of it. Some of us think that this will teach our kids a lesson 'once and for all'. All this does is to teach them to avoid being caught the next time, and to see apologizing as a humiliating and avoidable act.

⊛ Teach children to apologize as well as to accept apologies gracefully. If they have been wronged or slighted in some way, and you or another person offers a sincere apology, children are at times tempted to "milk" the situation by remaining angry and hurt. Demonstrate to them how pleasant and 'complete' the situation is, once an apology has been made and has been accepted. In short, teach them to forgive with grace too.

Teaching a child to make a genuine apology is a layered lesson. It teaches kids that goodness means, not only doing the right thing, but knowing what is the right thing to do after wrong behaviour.

b for boundaries

Confide in your children with caution; it may be too much of a burden for them.

"My daughter is my best friend. I can confide all my joys and hopes, and fears in her now," says the mother of a 13-year-old girl. As children grow and understand the more complex emotional and social issues of family life, it becomes easier for parents and children to become 'friends'. Children can be consulted on many family decisions, minor as well as major. It is indeed a wonderful feeling when your young child brings his or her new, fresh perspective to a discussion – be it about where to vacation, what colour to paint the home, what charity to get involved with, or how to sort out an awkward family situation.

However, a word of caution: keep some boundaries. Do not turn your children into your confidants and problem-solvers. Beyond a point, it becomes a strain on their young minds and lives.

Family issues/problems usually revolve around:

relationships, money, illness, and the like. Many parents ask: "Shouldn't our youngsters be given an idea of the reality around them, about family/financial problems? Doesn't this make them better people, to grow in empathy, and to take responsibility?"

The answer to that is yes, but a qualified yes. Of course your adolescent or teenaged children should have a realistic picture about their parents' financial situation, relationships, health, and such matters. However, they do not need to know every detail. This is because they are not adults, and cannot fully handle them on an adult level. And when they are called upon by us to do so, it requires them to draw too heavily on their mental and emotional resources, for which they are not yet equipped.

Drawing children into the intimate personal problems and conflicts between parents, or between parents and other adults in the family, should be avoided as far as possible. Constant references to loans, financial burdens, expenses, inflation, your savings/retirement plans, and the like do not serve really to give your youngster any real picture. Such conversations only serve to create anxiety. While you can expect your children to know and understand broader issues involved, try not to burden them with excessive details.

When it comes to inter-personal issues, while you may keep your child informed about important decisions, or points of disagreements in the family on a certain matter, never ask him or her to arbitrate or intervene between you and your spouse, or you and your in-laws, etc. This puts a grossly unfair burden on the child, forcing him or her into the lanes and byways of the adult world, for which he or she is not yet prepared. Having to contend with issues at this level only causes confusion, anxiety and even depression in children.

Unfortunately, many of us tend to 'lean' on our children in this way. Whether you are a single parent or a two-parent family or a joint family, you need other adults to talk to and seek advice from when it comes to your own anxieties or dilemmas. Your children can be taught to be understanding, empathetic and responsible; but for this they do not need to shoulder the burdens of the adult world.

b for bullying

Teach your kids how to tackle bullies — neither with violence nor with cowardice.

Kids face bullying at all ages. A 9-year-old boy who is not into games may be pushed around, called a sissy or a nerd, and generally teased to tears. A 14-year-old girl may be mercilessly targeted by her classmates for her choice of clothes, a 16-year-old boy may be boycotted by other boys because he refuses to indulge in eve-teasing. Parents often don't know whether they should step in and complain to the school or the bully's parents. At one level, you feel your child should learn to hold his or her own in such situations. And yet, stepping in on his behalf conveys that his family cares and will protect him. What is the right balance?

Particularly with boys, it is important that they learn to take some amount of bullying on the chin, ignore it, or even give back, measure for measure. Girls need to do this too, but the whole bullying-teasing thing seems to be more muted and not so merciless amongst girls at a young age.

Before stepping in (which you may have to do if it gets relentless or physical), you can help your children face bullies with a few strategies:

⚽ Ignoring the teasing. Which means not only to not respond, but to genuinely ignore it. This you can help him do by painting the teasers and bullies in a 'boring' light in conversations at home. Like they're a stuck record. Right now he sees them as his tormentors, as strong figures; if he sees them as silly fellows with nothing better to do, he may be able to ignore them better. It is a difficult concept for a 7 or 8-year-old to understand, but do try it.

⚽ Teasing right back. This is not in the tradition of 'Gandhigiri', 'turning the other check' no doubt, but a few smart come-backs which involve targeting some trait of the teasers may go a long way in getting the bullies to back off. While this is not something one likes to do, you might have to help your child actually find something to laugh at, about them, and thus go prepared with a little verbal 'ammunition'! Try to get him to do this in a kidding off-hand manner, and not in a battle-cry mode.

⚽ Agreeing with the teaser. One way to frustrate a teaser is to agree with whatever he says, in a bland or funny/absurd way. You could get him to say things like "Of course my shirt is funny, so what?" or "Ya I wore this just so that you could laugh; see how kind I am."

If the bullying takes the shape of really offensive name-calling or physical stuff, you just might need to step in at some point, and do three things, step by step.

⚽ Get the teacher in charge or principal to have a sensible

talk about bullying to the class/school in general –
particularly on the issue of studious students versus sports
lovers, and the pointlessness of the so-called 'divide'.

⚽ Take the intervention a step forward by calling up the
teasers' parents and having a calm and rational conversation
about this.

⚽ Casually drop in at end of a school day and address
some laughingly warning remarks to the teasers themselves.
For boys, preferably this should be done by both parents,
or the father alone. Because with boys, 'mama came to save
you' teasing can quickly follow.

While all this sounds like the stuff of strategic war
maneuvers, do try to carry them out as casually as possible,
so that your children can put bullying and teasing episodes
in perspective and move on with confidence.

C for Comparisons

Pointing to other children as 'good examples' serves no purpose – it only belittles your child.

Too many parents point out to other siblings, or other children, or their own childhood, when they want their child to improve or change. So often a parent will say: "Look at your younger sister – she never needs to be reminded to pack her bag for tomorrow," or "She never fusses about food,"…and other such examples. This may be your genuine reading, and also quite a puzzle to you – why does one child do certain things easily and the other need so much coaxing and prodding and bullying, you ask yourself. However, it is of little use when trying to get the other child to listen and behave.

Most children react to comparisons with some 'defence mechanism', such as ignoring what you're saying, or coming up with a sullen and unreasonable response like: "Well she does it because she's stupid" or "Because she's a goody-goody". So, in fact, your comparison has not only *not* worked, it has pushed the child further away from what you want him to do. Moreover, this could cause unhealthy rivalry between your kids.

When you compare a child with one of his friends or classmates, this too makes the child feel inadequate and resentful. "Why can't you be more like Sumit?" you ask your child in frustration sometimes, pointing out to some good quality in his friend. However much he likes his friends, this kind of comparison makes your child take defensive positions and perhaps come up with a list of 'bad' things that Sumit does. Or your child, stung by such a remark, will then come up with a long list of good things that he himself does (which Sumit never ever does), which you don't ever appreciate! Now the conversation has got emotionally derailed, and you are simply not able to get your point across.

As for the line "When I was your age I would always tidy the dining table/come first/eat well/study hard…" you can be sure that your children, most times, stop listening after the first five words!

While we may tell ourselves that we make such comparisons so that our child sees a positive example, the fact is that it almost never works that way. Comparisons of this kind don't work well, because they simply don't motivate. They judge, they find the child not measuring up, and they are left at that unhappy and rather hopeless note.

Of course we need to pull up our children at times and set them standards. But it is always much more positive and effective to compare a child *with his own potential*. When you say – "Look at how well you tidy up your room when you put your mind to it," or "Remember how polite and friendly you used to be till a few months ago?" – your child gets a positive mental image of himself, an example that he knows he has the potential to follow.

Your son or daughter simply has to feel that they are *valued for themselves*, as unique individuals who each have special qualities and talents. Only a genuine recognition of these qualities will motivate them to aspire to and realize their own potential. More importantly, only this kind of recognition and appreciation will ensure that they are willing to listen and be receptive to correction and suggestions for improvement from you.

"Comparisons are odious" it is said. Which means that comparing one thing to another, or for that matter, one child to another, is pointless - it robs the compared person of his or her core dignity, value and worth.

C for Counsellor

A counsellor can step in when the parent-child relationship needs support and direction.

In this age of nuclear urban families, many of us live without the parallel, compensatory support of the larger family unit within our homes. Without other adults and elders in the home, today parenting has become an extremely demanding, one-person or two-person task and responsibility. In addition to this, there are the stresses and strains of modern lifestyles, both on parents as well as children - work pressures, examinations, competition...

In this scenario, a counsellor has become an important and significant support-provider in the parent-child relationship.

What prompts people to go see a counselor? Several circumstances:

When the parent-child relationship has come to a difficult point, and there seems to be some kind of impasse, an inability to move forward.

🐞 When there is a persistent and recurring behavioural/ mental/emotional problem within the family unit or in school.

🐞 When parents/children experience overwhelming grief, anger, or confusion over an incident or a development.

🐞 When there is need for the intervention/help from outside of the family unit over a particular issue.

What does a counsellor bring to the situation? Many aspects:

🐞 A professional, objective and all-round understanding of the situation.

🐞 A compassionate approach, enabling both parent and child to voice their concerns, fears, or grievances.

🐞 An ability to identify, intervene and break any vicious cycle of behaviour that may have formed within the unit.

🐞 A limited, time-bound plan to effect sustainable change in the attitudes/behaviour of the people involved, and thus help them move forward.

What are the things that a counsellor will not/should not do? There are several:

🐞 Will not offer medication. Most counsellors are not trained/qualified to do so, unless they also have a degree in medicine/psychiatry. If a counsellor thinks that there is a psychiatric-medication issue involved, either with parent or child, she/he will refer them to a qualified psychiatrist.

🐞 Will not take the place of the parent – in teaching

children day-to-day good habits, helping with homework, or simply baby-sit for the parents.

⊛ Will not report to the parents everything that the child talks about or confides.

⊛ Will not 'gang up' with the parents and force the child to 'tow the line'. This means that the counsellor will not be necessarily the 'agent' of the parents.

⊛ Will not sit in moral judgement about anything that the child or parents reveal.

What should you tell your counsellor? Some key things:

⊛ First, visit without your child, and tell the counsellor whatever comes up, your own personal problems, your parenting issues, and any other matter that you may want to share.

⊛ Once you take your child, let your child speak, without interrupting him/her. The counsellor may also ask to speak alone with the child.

⊛ Always tell the counsellor the truth. It defeats the purpose to tell half-truths or exaggerations, or to hide an important family issue.

⊛ Go with an open mind, prepared to speak as well as listen, really listen. After all, you are not going there only to hear what you already believe. You are going to a counsellor for fresh insights.

There is an old saying: God can mend a broken heart – but you have to give him all the pieces. It is something like that with a counsellor.

C for Criticism

Genuine feedback, rather than harsh criticism, works wonders.

Criticism, by definition, is something that no one really likes to hear, particularly not children, and particularly not from their parents. However, we are often called upon to correct our children, and in the process to criticize them.

Firstly, why do we need to criticize, and not simply correct or guide a child each time that she errs in some way? We need to use criticism to show children (or anyone for that matter) not just their mistake, but a recurring tendency or attitude that needs to change. How do we do this in a way that is effective and yet not destructive or damaging to the child or to our relationship with her? Today there is a lot of talk about 'constructive criticism'. How does one criticize a child constructively?

By providing feedback, rather than judgement and condemnation of any particular behaviour. When you provide feedback, it checks you from making sweeping statements and drastic forecasts, such as: "you're **always** late" or "you're **never** going to learn". Feedback is milder, more to the point, and provides a cause-and-effect equation to the child. For instance: "You were late again today, this held up the school bus, and annoyed the other children. Soon they may ask you to come on your own to school." No doubt, when a child repeatedly makes the same mistake, we are sorely aggravated and tempted to say something quite nasty – but this is really only to vent our own feelings of irritation, and does nothing constructive at all.

Secondly, constructive criticism is always made with a suggestion (or even possibly a rule) about how something can be done differently. Take the example of the child who is late in getting ready for school. Suggesting and implementing earlier wake-up time, better preparation for school on the night before, etc work much better than your harsh words, however real and valid they may be. This takes the problem in a forward direction, instead of round and round, in predictable and frustrating circles.

Thirdly, constructive criticism is always genuine. So it is never couched in pretend-sweet words. You do not need to swing from being severe and harsh to being sugary on the surface – most children can see right through that kind of a thing! While providing constructive criticism, you can be kind, but firm and effective.

Last, and perhaps most important, as parents we need to step back and examine calmly and closely, the issues on which we consistently rebuke, criticize and often even ridicule our children. While some of them may be valid areas of concern, quite a few, on closer examination and introspection, are a result of us projecting our own fears, anxieties, failings, ambitions and even obsessions on to our children's lives.

A good thumb-rule to check your behaviour, in this
context, is: the nastier and more intense you are with your
child on a certain issue, it is most likely that this is a problem
area about which you need to look within. This much we
owe to ourselves and our children – to be able to distinguish
what a child really needs by way of life skills, and what is
simply irrational insistence on our part that things are done
only in a certain way, 'our' way.

d for discipline

One parent playing the Good Cop and the other playing Bad Cop isn't quite how disciplining works.

"My son thinks I am a wet blanket and spoil-sport, while his Dad is great fun and the kindest softy in the world," a mother complains. When it comes to matters of discipline with kids, it is usually one parent who ends up being the 'Hitler' or the 'villain of the piece'.

In this mother's case, as with a lot of other parents, somehow she has come to be the one who always has to say 'no' or to insist on bed-time being maintained or homework being finished, and a hundred other things that go into the making of a child's daily routine.

The father of the child, on the other hand, says that she is too strict and harsh, and so he needs to counter-balance things by always giving in and relaxing the rules and generally showing a kinder face to the child. "Otherwise, if we both rain down on him with so many rules and regulations, life will become a grim affair for the child, won't it?" asks this father. The mother counters this by saying: "Why then do I always have to be the one who plays 'bad guy'?"

Indeed this is a valid question. While it is to some extent a question of individual parenting styles and personalities, it seems counter-productive for one parent to be constantly the one who lays down the law and enforces it.

For one, a young child then associates all discipline and tasks and duties with one parent, and all fun-times with the other parent. Invariably, the child also takes forever to complete what one parent 'goes on and on' about; and instantly listens to any instruction or request from the more lenient parent. This further frustrates the 'bad guy' parent and in some households, the 'good guy' then even thinks that he is the 'better' parent. Secondly, this undercuts the authority of one parent. Children learn to 'wheedle' and negotiate their way out of situations by appealing to the 'good guy' parent, and the parent who has laid down certain rules is left looking silly as well as plain unkind, which is not the intention at all.

Parents simply have to share duties in matters related to discipline. One may have a certain way of doing it and the other may have a different way, but in essence both must come to an understanding about certain issues – for instance brushing teeth before bed – and insist that it is done. Far too often, one parent will try and get the child to do it by saying: "Hurry up and brush your teeth or your Mummy will get angry." And poor Mummy is obliged to play 'Hitler' even at bed-time!

In a slightly different scenario, one mother, who is a great perfectionist, insists that all disciplining is done by her. Even when the father does want to get involved and handle certain areas – for instance getting his 9-year-old daughter to pack her bag for school on the previous night – the mother insists that she herself must 'oversee the operation'. This too is a lopsided way of handling things, and often ends up with the other parent giving in or giving up. All too often the father then ends up saying "Ask Mama" when it comes to anything that involves asking for permission.

Disciplining children and inculcating good and regular habits is, at best of times, a demanding and complex task. Why not use the 'Power of 2' – so that it becomes easier for everyone concerned?

e for *e*motional Intelligence

Emotional Intelligence is the key to personal development, stable relationships and meaningful careers.

The world over, companies, organizations and nations are talking about collaboration rather than competition. On the family and personal front too, relationship-building is being recognized as the key to emotional well-being. In voluntary/ charity work too, empathy rather than sympathy, is truly effective. It takes Emotional Intelligence to be an active and fulfilled citizen of our world.

While for decades a high-IQ has been a much-sought-after and much-saluted mental feature, today a high EQ is being recognized as an important, even crucial, measurement of life skills. It is today a proven fact that people who perform well are those with high IQs as well as EQs – people with knowledge as well as understanding and wisdom.

This means that the definition of intelligence has been expanded: the truly intelligent are those who can absorb not just information, but knowledge; and one step beyond this, they have the wisdom to use what they know in ways that make their lives happy, fulfilled and socially connected.

While we stress so heavily on children's study habits, there is clearly a need for us to shape our children's emotional habits too, for them to become complete human beings. Good emotional habits – self-awareness, optimism, considerateness, to name just a few – can be taught to children, giving them a better chance to use their intellectual abilities well.

It is the interplay between our emotions and our intelligence that decides what we make of our lives. People who are simply taken over by emotions cannot be effective; on the other hand, those who use their intellect, without being able to read their own emotional needs and recognize the emotions of others, tend to lose out on all-round progress too.

Even when we wish to instill good moral and ethical standards in our children, when we want to teach them to be honest, tolerant, fair, kind; to manage their emotions like anger, frustration, jealousy, it is their emotional intelligence that needs to be awoken and sharpened.

While there are endless debates about whether intelligence is a genetic gift, or can be nurtured, the good news is that emotional intelligence can be taught, learnt, practiced and sharpened in children. Here, the school system rarely plays a role. It is the family that simply must impart this 'education'. The best way, of course, is by example. When children observe and experience their parents and other close family members dealing with their lives in an emotionally intelligent manner, this is the best lesson.

However, there are a couple of specific ways in which you could give your kids a small 'emotional workout':

🐞 Encourage 'feeling' conversations. When your child tells you about what happened at school or on the playground, get him to articulate what he felt, or what someone else in the interaction felt. This can be done as a natural part of the conversation, and not as a 'counselling session', though.

🐞 Get children to listen, to read and recognize people's tones and expressions, and not just their words; even the cats and dogs around them have expressions! Teach your kids to observe and interpret non-verbal communication too.

How often we have seen, looking back on our own school days, that kids in our class who were called 'scholars' – or 'nerds' in today's terms – did not go on to blaze any trails. What became of them – we wonder. While others, who were not necessarily on top of the class, or in the merit list, went on to become successful, happy, self-actualized people. The key ingredient in their upbringing was Emotional Intelligence.

e for excelling

Anxious to make achievers out of their kids, many parents are on gross overdrive.

Parents today are loading their kids with everything that they didn't have - opportunities, things, holidays, exposure.

They are putting out good money and ferrying kids to this coaching class and that camp, in the hope that they are preparing them for future competition, and teaching them lessons in application and achievement.

But in this overdrive to ensure that kids excel at everything they do, many are committing a grave parenting mistake: failing to prepare kids emotionally and mentally for the adult world.

By focusing so fretfully on giving children everything so that they can excel, what we are increasingly seeing are superficially well-developed children who are very often, actually, sad, lonely, confused and lack self-confidence because they haven't fulfilled parental expectations. Some of them may be depressed too, while showing no outer signs that the treadmill that you've put them on is just not working for them.

So while you may think you're giving your child a head start, you're actually ensuring that he/she will always be held back by deep-rooted self-doubt and fear of trying anything for fear of not excelling.

How will children 'dare to dream' if you set them a goal (your goal) before they even start? You may not spell it out to them, but children pick up on the fact that their parents are desperate for them to 'excel'. And some parents go right ahead and spell it out: "I paid an arm and a leg for that creativity camp and what do you have to show for it?"

So step back a little. It's great that you can give your kids all the exposure that you didn't have. Now have a little faith: that what you are doing may not give you quick and decisive 'results'. But it is definitely not 'wasted' – it all goes into the making of a child. That piano class may not lead her to become a performer, but it will no doubt get her to listen to music with a more evolved ear and enjoy it better. Maybe not now, but later in life, and for keeps. That will not go away. However, it definitely will, if the piano class is stuck sideways in her throat because of your expectations. So too with tennis, or football, or any other of the stuff that you take them for.

Take another step back. Think of how many of the things that you're hoping your kids excel in are actually what you wanted while growing up. Equally, how many of the fears you express on his behalf are actually your own anxieties? Sift through these thoughts, and you will then see your child as an emerging, forming individual, who cannot be constantly honed to perfection by you.

What you provide your kids simply has to be in your role as an enabler, not a puppeteer. This is an urgent change in perception that you need to put in place, or else you run the risk of your children dodging your grand schemes and choosing to do nothing. The primary thing is that your kids should enjoy thoroughly what they do. That sense of enjoyment and participation will feed their minds and souls far better than the 'excelling' that seems to be such a modern-day parenting password.

e for expectations

Beware of smothering your kids with your own hopes and fears.

We all have expectations from our children. These range from day-to-day behaviour, school performance, good habits, to what they make of their lives. Expectations can be a double-edged sword. People who grow up with their parents having realistic and positive expectations, are more likely to be emotionally stable achievers. Those whose parents had unrealistic and/or negative expectations, tend to be mal-adjusted, suffer from low self-esteem and an overall lack of direction.

When parents have realistic and positive expectations of their child, this means that they recognize a child's potential, create an enabling environment, and encourage the child to fully grow to his or her potential. For instance, if your child is musically inclined, you may have him learn music, buy him tapes and CDs, take him to music programs. You may encourage him to take part in public programs, competitions and the like. You watch his progress with interest and involvement, without getting attached to a pre-planned outcome about exactly where this interest in music will take him. If the child decides that it remains a serious hobby, you're ok with that; if he decides that he wants to pursue it professionally, you are ok with that too.

A parent who has unrealistic expectations, quickly jumps to a future scenario where the child simply must become a famous playback singer. Nothing less will do. This is a positive expectation, but is usually quite unrealistic, and leads to excessive pushing, future disappointments, blame, and many other negative situations, including putting the child off permanently from pursuing music.

Negative expectations are extremely destructive too. So many parents love to 'deflate' a child by saying: "You won't amount to anything. Why bother to study, anyway you're going to be sweeping the streets…" and other such comments. Some parents think this can 'shame' and 'goad' children into trying harder. This kind of negative labeling rarely does any such thing. And if it does, it is a kind of negative fuel that simply eats into the child. He may end up being an achiever, just to prove his parents wrong, but is bound to be an unhappy person, motivated by all kinds of negative emotions.

Also, while having expectations of your children is natural and good, it is counter-productive to have very specific expectations about their future: "My daughter will become a doctor." "My son will become a pilot." "My kids will get into an Ivy League college." "My child will never enter business; he is going to be an academic." The problem with such specific expectations is that they are often more to do with your own hopes and dreams than with what your child is all about.

When talking about their future, it is much more meaningful and encouraging for parents to talk to children about their potential, their many good traits, the opportunities open to them, the benefits of hard work, honesty... This way, you create an atmosphere of hope and the feeling that the world is open to them. What they do with this mix of positive things depends on every child's specific inclination, rather than a pre-planned script written by the parent.

Beware! Your expectations of your child are like self-fulfilling prophecies, and will shape their future. Keep them realistic and yet positive and check yourself from pouring your own past failures or unfulfilled wishes into your children's future.

f for farewells

Saying goodbye is never easy, but it doesn't have to be traumatic.

Saying goodbye, for all of us, is in varying degrees a sad experience. For children it is often traumatic. From their very first "tata" that we teach them, there are so many partings and farewells that they have to experience in their lives. The first sad and often traumatic 'bye is when a child has to experience being parted from a parent who leaves every day for work.

Most children get over their initial sense of loss and abandonment by having someone else – like a grandparent or nanny – to turn to at that moment, and mainly, by developing the faith that the departing parent is sure to return. This is the reassurance that we must provide and stick to as far as possible. A phone call sometime in the day helps greatly too, so that your child, whatever be his age, knows that he is in your thoughts, however demanding your job is.

In today's world of high mobility, people move

neighbourhoods, cities, countries, even continents, many times in their life. This generation of children is therefore dealing with so many more goodbyes than before – leaving relatives, friends, teachers and neighbours behind many times over. Kids need to be reassured and encouraged to stay in touch with people through email, letters and occasional phone calls too. This way, some level of continuity is maintained, and children learn to remain linked and invested in relationships instead of developing an overly 'here-today gone-tomorrow' approach to emotional ties.

The most painful farewells, of course, are those that kids must say when they encounter death. The loss of a grandparent, a favourite relative, a friend, a pet...all cause much pain, confusion, fear and even anger in children. It is absolutely essential that the child is allowed to grieve, and yet provided with a kind of base-support to provide a bottom to her anguish. Gently, at appropriate times, the child can be led through the process of such a loss, so that she understands the inevitability of it and yet learns to believe that whatever she had with the person/pet is in no way lost or negated by death.

Here are some dos and donts that will help you see your child through separation or loss of any kind:

✪ Explain the situation, but do avoid being overly rational and wordy. Sometimes, silences provide the best reassurance and empathy.

✪ Don't be in a hurry to have your child 'get over' the loss. Let him stay with the feeling, and in this way acknowledge to himself that a relationship is/was precious.

⚽ Sometimes children appear casual and offhand when they have to say goodbye. Don't mistake this for insensitivity. They are struggling with feelings inside, and give them the space and time for this.

⚽ Do avoid insisting that children say goodbye only in a format that you prescribe ("give your aunt a hug," "say bye, I'll miss you", and other such instructions.)

⚽ Calm feverish imaginations – many children fear the worst when their parents come home even a little late – by calling them up if you're delayed. Avoid telling them about a near-accident you may have had on the way back or about some accident that you saw, etc.

⚽ When dealing with death, find ways to teach your child to hold on to the essence of the departed person – the good feelings and memories, so that the sense of loss is not irreparable and devastating.

All cultures talk about life as a journey. Let us help our children deal with the many terrains, co-passengers, arrivals and farewells that they will encounter on theirs.

g for godparents

Encourage your kids to bond with other adults – and watch them grow in many more dimensions.

We live in increasingly 'nuclear' times, especially in urban India. Joint families – especially the 'tightly' joint together families of the past – are now rare. Family sizes too have grown smaller and families have scattered. And so, children today are not likely to have too many relatives – just a couple of aunts and uncles and a few cousins, a couple of grandparents, and those too not necessarily in the same town or city.

Meeting and interacting with them is restricted to a few holidays here and there, if at all. True, today instead of a close network of cousins, kids have friends and classmates. What kids have lost out on, however, in this situation, is the sustained presence of significant, loving, responsible and fun adults *other than their parents*.

We've all had one at least – that favourite aunt or uncle, grandparent or godparent, who loved us quite unconditionally. Who would indulge (not necessarily spoil) us, laugh at our jokes again and again, whose freezer always had ice-cream, who'd tell us about the mysteries of the Universe, come up with solutions to offbeat problems, or listen to some of our complaints about our parents as we grew – and even play mediator at times.

These are the godparents or para-parents of our lives. They're the ones who'll generally hang loose with kids without having the weighty duties of 'being a parent'. In no way do they replace parents, but they play an essential role in the emotional growth of a child. They're important people in the life of a child's parents too. They're the safety-valve when the parenting pressure builds up.

Given that such a person is not 'available' quite easily and naturally from within the larger family anymore, parents need to go out of their way to encourage and nurture such relationships.

Why are para-parents important?

❀ They broaden the relationship-base of a child. The child at first knows the adult only in the form of its parent – this interaction is bound up with issues of love, trust, nurture, reward, punishment – hands-on, 24/7, as they say. For a child to learn to know and trust other adults, learn to give and take, it is essential that he interact closely with adults other than his parents.

❀ Children often feel deeply frustrated by the 'decisions and rulings' of their parents. The presence of a 'Third Umpire' in a child's life is crucial – it gives him/her a sense of fairness from the adult world. If this Third Umpire supports the parent's decision in some matter, the child is able to take it better. The Third Umpire is also able to intervene on behalf of the child at times, if the parent is being unnecessarily harsh or unreasonably demanding.

⬤ When we punish our children, we tend to not just punish them for their 'crime' but to severely criticize and reject their entire personality for a while, in our anger and anxiety to correct their behaviour. The para-parent, at such times, is available to the child as a person who, again, may support the parent in the disciplinary action, but is detached enough from the situation to not reject and shun the child totally. For the child, this is an assurance that he/she is not an utterly bad and unlovable person.

⬤ Many parents tend to over-focus on their children, overprotect them and in this way limit their experience of the world, in their anxiety to bring up a perfect child to whom no harm ever comes. The para-parent, in this scenario, is a more relaxed adult figure, with whom the child is safe and yet able to explore; looked after and yet not excessively fussed over.

Who makes a good para-parent?

⬤ Any mature, loving human being from the age of 21 to 101, who the child, as well as parent, likes and trusts.

⬤ A person who has time and energy to be in the child's life in a sustained fashion. Continuity and dependability is very important for kids – and a mere Santa Claus who appears once a year bearing gifts is *not* para-parent material.

⬤ A person who does not hold a world-view and lifestyle

too dramatically different from those of the parents. This can be too confusing for a child.

⊛ And yet, not a person who is a clone of the parent either. A para-parent who's a little different form the parent has so much more to offer a child, bringing in refreshing new ideas, emotions and experiences. The Para-parent is *not* just a substitute parent.

⊛ One who is not over-eager to 'mould' and 'guide' children, but one who, by the way he/she chooses to interact with the child, builds respect and affection.

A note of caution: For a healthy bond to form between an adult and a Para-parent, firstly, the parent has to know and believe that this adult in no way displaces the parent or undermines his/her authority. There is no place for jealousy and rivalry between two adults over a child – that would be an emotional disaster, the brunt of which is borne by the child in the form of guilt and emotional confusion.

Parenting is a demanding career – and growing up is hard work too, for kids. Make it a little easier and more interesting by enlisting the aid of a para-parent!

g for grandparents

Respect and affection for the elderly makes a better person out of a child.

The media – TV serials, films, advertisements – that children see, often portray old people in an extreme light: As either grouchy, nasty, forgetful; or as angelic, beautiful, ever-smiling. Neither of these images treat the elderly as real people. Neither of these images are a reflection of reality at all. At a certain level, this affects the way children and youngsters behave with the elderly.

Today, many parents and grandparents complain that their children, especially after the age of 6 or 7, show no respect or concern for the old people in their family. Even if they are not out-and-out rude, they tend to ignore the elderly, make no special time for them, and show impatience and irritation towards them.

Common complaints from children are: "Ajji lectures too much; Dada keeps repeating herself; Ajoba walks too slowly; Mothi-aai takes too much time over something;

Nana snores too loudly; Nani keeps asking me to do chores" and so on and so forth.

The situation calls for a 3-generation understanding of one another. All three sets of people need to let go a little, as well as insist on certain protocols or rituals that simply have to be carried out, if old people are not to be marginalized and cast aside once their 'use' in the family is over.

◉ Parents need to keep their criticisms of their own parents to themselves, and avoid having children 'in' on old, long-standing quarrels. However, grandparents too need to avoid gossiping or complaining to grandchildren about their parents. This kind of pulling of the child in two directions only serves to confuse kids and to encourage them to ignore what both sets of adults say!

◉ Parents need to insist that children maintain a certain degree of respect and thoughtfulness towards the grandparent, and continue to make time for them. However, sometimes a grandparent too needs to learn to let go a little, and accept that children's lives are full and busy, and it is in the nature of things that they run far ahead.

◉ Parents need to listen when children complain about a grandparent's possibly irritating habit – like snoring heavily, or being neglectful of bodily hygiene, or using the bathroom in a messy way, and other such things. There is no point simply telling children to shut up when they voice their irritation or ask searching and potentially embarrassing questions. However, children have to be taught to put up with it to some degree – not because they have no choice, but because these things are a natural part of ageing. This may be difficult for a child to understand and accept, but we need to make that effort.

If we ourselves remember that elders have a special contribution to make to the family, inspite of failing physical or mental health, our children too will value this and learn to accept the other possibly troublesome aspects of an ageing person's presence.

If we deal with old age and ageing as a life-stage rather than some kind of disease, our children too will learn to deal sensitively, lovingly and with compassion with the old people in their family.

g for guilt

Psychologists as well as spiritual guides emphasise: one of the foremost 'fuels' of unhappiness and mental ill-health is guilt.

Most of us, as children, and young adults, have experienced guilt, and continue to do so. Sometimes it is 'good guilt' – for some wrong we have done, or for something that we ought to have done. It may be guilt about not exercising enough, or not spending enough time with our families, or not concentrating on work, etc. This kind of guilt is motivating, and can be 'fixed' by whatever is clearly needed to be done: apologizing, making amends, changing some behaviour, fixing a schedule and adhering to it, etc. In such situations, our guilt works constructively.

The more destructive and dangerous, 'bad guilt' is the kind we carry around over issues that we wrongly identify as our 'fault'. Often it is about circumstances over which we have no control, yet we feel guilty. The accumulation of this kind of guilt begins from childhood, even from infancy. It then casts its long shadows on our later lives, not allowing us to self-actualize, to stand up for ourselves, to identify what we want from life, or to simply take pleasure in life.

Parents, anxious to teach their children to learn responsibility, often confuse 'good' with 'bad' guilt. They end up using guilt or emotional blackmail, to get their children to do things eat, study, earn, make career and marriage choices...

Let's look at an everyday example. Your child repeatedly forgets to pack her pencil box in her bag. Fed-up of this, you stop reminding her and let her face the consequences. She side-steps the problem by simply borrowing a pencil from someone in school. She does this once too often, and her friend/teacher snaps at her and tells her to get her own pencil. She now feels guilty about her carelessness and about not listening to your reminders, and now makes it a point to take her pencil box. This is good guilt at work.

However, on the other hand, if you were to repeatedly rush after her to school and hand the pencil box to her, and then berate her at home about how you had to waste time and energy for something that she should have done herself, she feels guilty, but her behaviour simply doesn't change. She keeps forgetting the pencil box, you find ways to get it to her or to nag her in the morning about it, even telling her how frustrating and irritating you find this. She grows up with a vague sense of unease about how she annoys her mother, and has caused her mother all kinds of hardships. The actual pencil box incidents are forgotten, and only a harmful, free-floating guilt takes its place in later years.

Some sources of guilt that parents can watch out for:

'Bad guilt' accumulates when lines of communication

between parent and child are weak. It is a well-documented fact that many children of divorced parents carry around a burden of guilt, as if somehow it was their fault. Only when the parent can recognize this train of thought, can he or she intervene and set the record straight, freeing the child of his guilt.

Another source of guilt is when children don't know how to handle strong feelings – anger, sexual attraction, etc. Parents need to communicate to them that it is ok to feel anger, but not ok to act on it (for instance, hitting or shouting at friends). Or that it is ok to feel attracted to a boy, but not ok to act out these feelings.

Sometimes parents live through their children, neglecting their own lives, and keep emphasizing how they have sacrificed their own careers/social life/needs...etc for their kids. This is another tonne of guilt that the child then has to carry, without being able to do anything about it. This kind of guilt leads children to be, at an unconscious level, almost apologetic about living, something that will completely prevent them from realizing their best potential.

h for harmony

Children thrive when there is harmony and hope in the home.

"He's fast asleep" "she's too small to understand" "he didn't hear anything"…how often as adults we convince ourselves that our children are not in any way affected by adult fights/arguments/unpleasantness. In fact we tell ourselves that if an incident of this kind did not take place right in front of a child, then he hasn't even registered it, so where's the question of being affected by it.

This is simply not true. If we go back a little into our own childhood, all of us can remember feeling that tight knot of tension in the stomach, when there was a problem between our parents or other adults in the house. You may have heard out-and-out yelling or bickering or gossiping; or you may have heard nothing at all, but picked up on all kinds of non-verbal clues that clearly indicated to you, that all was not well.

It is now so well-established that infants, even embryos, are affected by moods, tones, nuances and actions of the adults in whose care they are. Why then do we tell ourselves that our kids won't know anything about us unless they're actually told? It is time we fully recognized that our children are deeply affected by even the unsaid and unexpressed in the household.

Of course, every family has its ups and downs, rifts, reconciliations, arguments. What is significant, is how these are handled, and how they come across to your kids. If adult relationships around a child are basically good, strong, respectful and trusting, then a child is able to take a certain degree of disagreement, raised voices, or unhappy silences in his or her stride. It is when fights in the household signal that there is an absence of love and mutual trust and respect between the adults, that a child begins to be badly affected.

Children today are brought to doctors and counsellors for depression, lack of concentration, slow physical growth, eating disorders. Most people tend to lay the blame on 'outside distractions' – TV, video games, fast food, and other such externals. However, in at least 7 out of 10 cases, there is a fairly serious relationship problem that the child is 'witness' to in the household. Again, there may be nothing openly wrong, but there are often undercurrents of discord, that play a key role in unsettling a child and make him or her vulnerable to all kinds of disorders, emotional and physical. The adults in a house may individually shower a child with attention, facilities, love, praise... And yet, if the interpersonal relationships between these adults are unpleasant, even covertly so, much of what is showered on the child simply slides away, not nourishing him at all. After all, a tree cannot bloom however much of fertilizer you feed it, if the basic supply of soil, sun and water is not assured.

Children simply thrive on harmony and hope; and if these are often absent in their homes, their spirit shrivels. No amount of 'pretend happiness' between adults ever fools a child. We simply have to provide them the real thing by working genuinely on our own relationships.

I for Imagination

Give your children the space and time to imagine…and watch their creativity flourish.

If someone hadn't imagined it, we would never have had planes, electricity, the Ajanta paintings, the Qutub Minar, great stories. Invention, creativity, inspiration, discoveries… they have all been fuelled by people who have used their imagination. Or one should say, by people whose imagination was allowed to flourish freely.

Today, our children seem to have too little time to imagine. Between school work, home work, classes, TV, video games, where is the scope for a child to simply be, and to let his imagination entertain him? Earlier, with much fewer sources of passive entertainment (TV and video games) and knowledge-gathering (the internet, CDs) available, children simply had to actively use their imagination to find amusement as well as to discover how things worked.

Along with a good education, access to hobbies, vacations and entertainment, we simply must gift our children the time and space to play and work with their imagination. Sadly, for decades now, the Indian school child's introduction to the world of art is through a prescribed, rigid subject: draw a rainy day. It's the same with writing: write about your holiday. And down the decades, the contents of these paintings and essays simply don't change. As long as there are raincoats, dashes of blue crayon signifying rain, the child has drawn 'correctly'. As long as there is mention of a journey, some monument...we are satisfied – our child has 'completed' the essay on her holidays.

This way, there is simply no scope or encouragement given to 'think out of the box'. While in actual fact, most children notice and respond to the most unusual and great variety of things on a rainy day or on their vacation – things that escape the notice of most adults. And, most importantly, a child does not have to even go anywhere, or actually experience something, to come up with an imaginative set of impressions.

The two run-away successes – Lord of the Rings and the Harry Potter series – are indeed a refreshing return to imagination. However, they are still passive forms of entertainment, and are not a substitute for nurturing our own kids' imagination. Children's imagination needs an outlet. It used to be a natural process at one time, since they dreamt-up games and inventions, magical places and people. Today, when they are forced to be constantly rational, focused and real, and even worse, constantly fed pre-digested fun and information, they are in danger of getting bored, understimulated, and even depressed.

One mother complained that she 'caught' her 12-year-old daughter making odd climbing hand-movements in the air.

When asked what she was doing, the child guiltily said 'nothing'. This made the mother even more anxious, convinced now that her child was behaving 'abnormal'. Finally, at the end of the day, the child revealed that she had just been trying to imagine what it would be like to walk vertically – like a spider or a lizard. She had been trying to imagine the feeling, as well as the technicalities: which leg goes first, then which follows, etc! But the whole episode was seen in the house as 'crazy' behaviour.

Let's give our children some credit – of being creatures with far more joy, curiosity, humour and imagination than us adults! And let's nurture these qualities instead of 'straightening them out'.

I for Interrupting

Teach you kids the natural rules, the give and take, of a real conversation.

Recently, some visitors to India from a western country commented, with some amusement and a little annoyance – "Indians are like children; they really have to interrupt you while you're talking, the minute a thought strikes them."

Yes indeed, we do. We constantly interrupt each other at family conversations, at parties, even in discussions. Watch any so-called debate on TV, and you'll see that no one ever lets the other complete his thought or sentence. This is not just a question of ill-manners, it is also a real impediment to good communication. This means we are often not willing to listen or to dialogue. This is a serious put-off in any interaction, and as we go increasingly global, we need to teach our children how not to interrupt. So that they become more attuned to the way people communicate in a group.

This does not mean, of course, that we tell children to

simply 'shut up and sit down' or 'be seen and not heard' while adults are conversing. We need to teach them to 'wait their turn' in a conversation, by looking for a natural break or lull before they cut in. Or we can teach them to use other ways to indicate that they would like to say something. For them to be able to accept and practise this, they must be made to feel that they will get their time and chance to add to a conversation or ask a question.

What really doesn't work at all is a scenario that goes something like this: You're talking to someone, your child keeps trying to interrupt and say something; you neither reply nor tell him to wait. He increases his volume, maybe even begins to pull at your clothes, or your face. All the while you're half-listening to the other person, and then finally you yell at the kid: "OK, What is it?" Now you have taught him that interrupting is fine, and his being loud and insistent works even better!

The other scenario that is a no-no too, goes something like this: You're trying to have a conversation with someone. Your child interrupts. You immediately cut the person who's talking to you, and attend to the child's question or comment. Then you go back to your conversation. Again the child interrupts, again you dump the conversation. Now you've taught your child that nothing is more important than what she has to say or wants, at all times, and simply cannot wait.

Children, by the age of 5-6, can be gently told that certain things need your immediate attention, while other things can wait. Teach your child to say "Excuse me" or "I want to say something," or some words or sign to indicate that he has something to say. And once you do ask him to speak, do give him your full attention, and encourage others in the room too to listen and not interrupt or complete his sentence for him.

And as with almost all matters of good parenting, teach by example. Watch your own behaviour, and see how often you interrupt people or barely wait for them to finish what they're saying, so that you can jump in with what you want to say. Once you've checked yourself, you'll be in a much better position to hold a meaningful conversation…and your kids will learn not to be Interrupting Indians too!

j for jealousy

Sibling rivalries are inevitable, but they can be kept in perspective.

While we all struggle to be impartial and fair to our kids, this can be extremely difficult, what with them being at different ages/stages, having different personalities with differing needs. On top of it is the dynamics between two siblings, which you have to take into account too, especially when there is a slightly large age gap between the older and the younger.

Many older children, suddenly finding themselves hardpressed to share parental love and attention with a younger child that has 'shown up', have been known to say things like: "I told you we should have got a puppy instead." Or "Why can't we send him back to God?" and other similar heart-felt sentiments. (There's a book on the subject of sibling rivalry that is actually titled: *I'd Rather Have an Iguana*, by Heidi Stetson Mario.)

Parents try to find a balance, but sometimes it just doesn't work. While you may be feeling that you're being fair, your older child often feels pushed around and treated unfairly on account of the younger one.

To start with, don't discourage your older child from honestly expressing what's on her mind, at least to you, in private. When she says nasty things about her younger brother or sister in front of the small child, you would usually say things like: "What a terrible thing to say! You don't really hate your sister... You have to be more caring, you're older." This forces her to push her feelings underground, where they build up steam. Instead, give her a chance to vent, to you.

By limiting her aggressive responses to the younger child, but permitting the expression of aggressive thoughts and feelings, you'll actually diminish sibling rivalry, in the long run. Respond to her complaints with genuine understanding. For instance: "I know you're very angry with Baby because she grabbed your origami. She's too young to understand how hard you worked on it. But I promise I'm going to try harder to keep her out of your way." And do seriously see to it, visibly and demonstratively, that Baby too begins to learn to respect Didi's things.

Some parents even go so far as to share a secret humourous/comical moment with their older child, when the younger one is being particularly bothersome, but needs to be accommodated at the moment.

Sometimes young siblings can get into pretty rough physical fights too. Though the fist-fest you witness between your kids may not seem like it, a whole lot of emotional and social processes are being put in place during this time, quite naturally, and at an early stage: sharing of parental love and attention, developing patience, dealing with irrationality/ unfairness, caring and responsibility, and other such issues. Many corners are rounded off during the growing years, consciously as well as unconsciously. This prepares children to deal later with the outside adult world of co-operative living, team work, sharing of resources, relationship building, social skills, putting up with idiosyncrasies etc.

However, it can be quite trying for a parent to constantly play referee and third umpire during these friendly and not-so-friendly 'matches', so you could try one simple device, that one parent has honed to perfection: 'go deaf' and 'become invisible' the minute they come up to you for arbitration and intervention! Simply refuse to engage. Get involved only if there is any chance of serious physical damage to life, limb or property (which a fight between two boys can quickly escalate into). For bickering, name-calling, grabbing space/stuff, arguing over what to play and who said what to whom, become totally unavailable.

There will be a longish phase, of several years, when your kids will truly feel that they dislike each other deeply. However, rest assured that they can't do without each other. While things do sort themselves out between siblings, parents need to do their bit too. Sibling relationships have much to do with how we feel about ourselves, as well as how we relate to others throughout our lives.

k for kindness

Teach kids to become truly generous, charitable and compassionate.

At a young people's party at a ritzy venue, the compere announced that 10 per cent of the proceeds of the entrance-ticket collection would be sent to flood relief work. The youngsters merely clapped, and went on partying. Now they did not need to think anymore about the flood victims – it was as if their conscience was clear. They had 'done their bit' towards charity. But this is not charity at all, really.

Whenever there is some disaster, coverage on TV of victims, relief work and charity coming in from all around; many children are caught up in the spirit of caring and sharing. This is an ideal time for parents to clarify their own thoughts and feelings about the issue of charity and giving.

While it is admirable and necessary that we respond to disasters, it is equally important that we instil in our kids the need to be charitable, at all times. What does this mean? It means that we need to teach our kids to respond to people's needs around them, not only to overwhelming disasters and crisis. It means that we teach our kids to, at times, put their own needs and wants aside, and take a good look at the less-privileged around them.

This does not mean that we take away from them the joys of owning toys, books, taking vacations. It does not mean that we make them feel guilty for enjoying what they have. But it does mean that we teach them to take others into account, and to become genuine, generous givers.

Again, generosity and giving does not only mean giving money. It's important that children understand that charitable acts do not always mean donating money. Volunteering their time or talents is a precious gift that your kids can bestow. It not only helps them become better people, but in the long-run, it changes the community around them. In this kind of giving, a child learns the essential life skill of giving of herself or himself, rather than simply giving what they don't need or have in surplus.

A mother complained that her 14-year-old son "is too helpful". He is very bright, she said, so "people waste hours of his time asking him maths and science difficulties. We keep telling him that he should concentrate on his own studies, and tell people to ask the teachers to sort out their problem."

It seems that too many of us have this kind of 'scarcity mentality' – that does not allow us to give freely of ourselves – because we assume that the resources are limited, and we will be depriving ourselves by helping others! So we end up giving away only what we can't use. That is not charity or generosity. It is simply a way of throwing away things and feeling good about it!

If we do want our kids to be real contributors to society, we need to communicate to our kids that helping others is not a duty; it's an opportunity: A chance to connect with people and their needs, a chance to be grateful for what you have, and a chance to differentiate between your own need and your greed. Indeed, appropriate charity gives us so many lessons in life itself.

And how do we communicate all this to our kids? The best way to do it, of course, is to set a good example with our own deeds. 'Caring is caught, not taught.' Give of yourself, in whatever little way you can, and your children will absorb the essence of your act. It is one of the greatest gifts that you can give them.

L for Letting Be

Most kids today are far too supervised – their time is accounted for, minute-to-minute.

We have become a majorly activity-oriented society, both adults and children. There seems to be no scope to simply sit, or potter around aimlessly, or doodle idly. All these are seen as a 'waste of time'.

In our bid to be conscientious and efficient parents, many of us are attached to the notion that everybody should be either busy or asleep!

Besides the studies and mundane daily activities that our children have to do, we also push them into 'creative activities' – again, for a supervised, regulated and clearly demarcated time. While this may be enjoyable for kids, it doesn't necessarily translate into enhanced creativity, or relaxation, for that matter.

Creativity as well as relaxation needs *vacant* space, where the mind is allowed to run in meandering directions, and not all of them 'fruitful' in any immediate sense. We send our kids to a creativity workshop, and they come home with maybe a painting/collage/picture frame and such things. We send them to, say, cricket coaching, so that they get a break from studies and get the benefit of sports activities. But we rarely give them the *vacant* space to simply stare into space and imagine up things, or *'aimlessly'* bounce a ball against a wall.

Remember the time, as kids, we enjoyed the simple activity of bouncing a rubber/tennis ball between our palm and the ground without a break? Remember 'playing around' with different kinds of lettering or doodles on paper? This was not 'sport' or 'creativity' in the modern sense of the term, but it no doubt was relaxing, enjoyable, and yes, may have even enhanced hand-eye co-ordination, drawing skills, etc.

Today we are terrified of our kids being bored. But boredom, one could say, is the mother of invention! How many interesting and imaginative games, activities, jokes, projects and conversations have emerged from the fact that a bunch of children are 'bored' in their holidays and have to invent a way to have fun.

Today, we complain that kids day-dream or lack focus during school hours. One of the reasons for this to happen is that children are so over-supervised at home, their time is so completely accounted for, that some of them find it easier to 'disconnect' in school, in a class full of other kids, when they can be physically present, but no one will notice that their minds have wandered off. Day-dreaming, lack of concentration, distracted behaviour, then become the common complaints from parents as well as teachers.

Perhaps we need to 'let out children be' — so that their

natural instincts for exploration, discovery, invention, creation, enjoyment and relaxation rise to the surface and flood their minds and bodies.

for lying

One of the most challenging tasks of parenting is teaching children not to lie.

From the age of 3 or 4, right till as late as 18, or even 20, children and young adults choose to lie their way out of a situation, and parents wonder how they can teach them the value of telling the truth.

Children lie for a variety of reasons. They lie to gain approval from parents, they lie so that they won't get in trouble, they lie to cover inadequacy. Some young children also lie because they don't make the clear distinction between fact and fiction.

What can we do to help children stop lying and to choose truth? Firstly, we have to make them experience truth telling as a tangibly good thing, rather than an abstract virtue. For this, there are a few things that we can do to facilitate telling the truth and discourage lying:

✺ Ease up: Kids sometimes lie because they feel they're not meeting our expectations, and it's easier to lie than feel like a failure. We need to, at such a time, take a good look at how we respond to our child's errors or failings. If we leave a little room for imperfections, chances are that our children will need to lie less to us.

🌑 Avoid 'awfulizing': Once you have found out that your child has lied about something, it is very tempting to lecture them, and in our anxiety to correct this behaviour, we tend to 'awfulize' the consequences of their lying, projecting into the future, warning them that they will turn into criminals, be shunned, be mistrusted, and so and so forth. This kind of huge canvas on which we paint this awful picture leaves the child confused and disconnected from the immediate reasons and consequences of his or her lie.

🌑 Focus on rectifying: Underscore the fact that admitting a mistake/error rather than lying about it, increases the chances of fixing the problem quickly – whether it is a lost notebook, lies told at school, stealing, breaking something… the entire gamut of things that kids lie about. Avoid getting stuck on blame and insisting on confessions, as this is traumatic and exhausting for both you and your child. Focus on sorting out the consequences and move on.

For instance, even if your child insists that he didn't break a lamp, you can simply say: "But it has broken, and we have to find a way to fix it." Then insist that the child be involved, even if it means foregoing a favourite TV program to go to the repair shop or to fix it at home. This way, you're not stuck at the spot where you want the child to say the words: "Yes I did it." You move beyond, where without much verbalizing, the child has to accept responsibility for his actions.

✪ Follow through: Sometimes we are so desperate for children to tell the truth, that we say: "If you tell the truth, you won't be punished." Letting kids off the hook once they accept a mistake, is only half the job done. You don't have to rub his nose in his errors, but getting him to make amends, in any small way, completes the lesson, and makes him feel good about himself again, and gives you a chance to give him that hug that he needs.

Demonstrate by your own actions and with lying episodes that take place in your household, that truth is light and easy to wear, while lies are a heavy and unpleasant burden to carry. Only then will kids grow up to actively choose the truth on their own, without being 'policed'.

m for mealtimes

There is an unstated, deeply beneficial aspect to family meals — food for body and soul.

In the last few decades, one aspect of family life that children have simply lost out on, is sit-down, everyone-together meals. It's time we 're-invested' in this simple family interaction, making time for at least one meal a day together. Family meal times are associated with healthier diets, even better absorption of nutrients. You'll be surprised at what far-reaching effects this has on your kids' emotional and physical health, social skills, and overall well-being. Pleasant meal-times together play a pivotal role in preventing various digestive and eating disorders — which have reached epidemic proportions amongst the young.

The unstated warmth and togetherness of a family meal can begin right from the kitchen, with the family helping with small tasks in putting the meal together. Laying the table (something of a ritual in most traditional cultures) itself sets the mood of care and love around a meal. It prepares mind and body, setting gastric juices flowing, and drawing your attention to the meal to come instead of a hundred other distractions.

Sitting down together for a meal ensures, quite naturally, that much considerate behaviour comes into play. Simple things: like eating without spilling or making chewing sounds, seeing that there's enough for everyone else before serving yourself, passing food to the other people, etc. All the stuff for which today we seem to need 'finishing schools' to teach our kids, but which can so easily be learnt right at the table!

One thing that can mar this potentially wonderful family interaction is what we choose to talk about or communicate during meal times. The entire interaction can become an uncomfortable one, if we use this time together to bicker or sort out unpleasant personal issues.

Some typical scenarios that we're all familiar with:

⚅ At the dinner table, Dad uses the fact that he's sitting face-to-face with his kids, to ask them about school work, marks, exams...If there's nothing great to report, the children side-step the question, or reluctantly reveal their school progress. Needless to say, the child has stopped paying attention to the meal, leave aside enjoying it. Others around the table are tense too. The family meal has been emotionally hijacked.

⚅ The family is at breakfast. Mom is issuing instructions to the maid, checking if some work has got done, asking Dad if he can make it for some appointment in the evening; Grandpa has some comment to make – the three of them get into a minor argument. All this while, food is being consumed – but it is food that's soaked in a gravy of grumbling. Hardly the stuff of health and well-being.

It's lunch time. The family is eating. In complete silence. Everyone is totally preoccupied with their own lives, plans and worries. They are only physically present around the table. As they finish, each person simply gets up from his or her seat and 'exits' the meal – as indifferently as one exits a computer program. The meal has turned into a joyless affair.

Another meal. Kids are pushing around food half-heartedly. Mom's exhausted, resentful, and announced that she's too tired to eat, after having 'produced' a meal. Dad's on the phone, conducting business, walking around with maybe a rolled *chappati* in his hand, perhaps a drink. Both parents are intermittently urging their kids to 'eat well' and 'finish everything on your plate'. The kids wish the food would somehow magically vanish. Someone gives them a lecture on how there are millions of starving children in our country, and they should be grateful to have food on their plate, for which their Mom has slogged. This mealtime is one of those dreary affairs, nicely garnished with guilt.

There are countless such scenarios. However, there are also innumerable ways in which we can make the family meal a real joy and the basis of our well-being. Whatever religion, faith or spiritual belief you have grown with or adopted, each and every culture and family has traditionally emphasized the sanctity of food and 'breaking bread' with your loved ones. Let's reconnect to that profound and pleasurable act.

m for money

The good things of life are free, actually.

We're all being constantly told, 'the good things in life cost money' (or a credit card). Increasingly, through the decades, the emphasis has been mainly on entertainment that money can buy: vacations, camps, sports gear, toys, clothes, special classes…

A parent mentioned how, when he decided to take his son out for a small drive, the 6-year-old asked as they were getting into the car: "Took your wallet?" Our children are growing up with the notion that no fun can be had without an exchange of money. Surely we need to bring some of the pleasure of just 'hanging loose' to our kids? After this incident, the child's parents decided that once a week would be a 'wallet forgotten at home outing'.

It takes only a little extra effort on our part to come up with fun trips or activities that do not involve spending money.

Let's look at just a few 'leads':

✾ Every season, your city has some tree or the other in bloom. Simply walk down to the nearest one with your child, and fill a whole basket with flowers or seeds, seed-pods shed on the ground. You'll be pleasantly surprised at how engrossed a child can get in this activity.

✾ Take a walk up a low hill or the seashore with your kids, and pick up a fascinating array of stones or shells – there's a treasure trove there. Come home, scrub them clean with your kids, and watch them sparkle in a tray or an artistic pile at the entrance to your home. Again, absolutely free.

✾ Involve your kid in any minor repair/maintenance work you're doing on your vehicle, instrument, or any part of your home. Even something as simple as oiling the hinges of a creaky door. Plan for it with enthusiasm and it won't be a chore but a fun activity, full of unspoken lessons.

✾ Revive indoor games, like good old carom, card games, and the like.

✾ Involve your child in gardening – even a little window-sill garden fascinates every child.

✾ Get a good storyteller – a relative, a friend – to narrate to your kids.

✾ Draw your child into cooking/baking.

There's so much that money just can't buy. Go get it for your kids!

Delve into your own childhood, and you'll recall that there were many such engrossing things that your parents did with you, which were not strictly speaking 'scheduled' children's 'entertainment'.

Of course, all this assumes that as a parent, grandparent or godparent you are willing to invest other important and more complex resources in your child besides money: time, energy and imagination. It also assumes that you yourself do not always need the props and distractions of shops, technology and merchandise to entertain and engage you in the many wonders that the world has to offer.

n for no

How to say 'No' without having a mutiny on your hands?

It's a tiny little word. It looks innocent enough. Just two letters and one simple syllable. But it's causing havoc in the home. Parents today are hard pressed to find ways to use it effectively and with as little damage as possible. And children today can go ballistic as soon as they hear it. It's the word 'No'.

Perhaps a cartoon of the 50s sums it up. It shows a 6-year-old boy introducing himself and his toddler sister to a visitor: "My name is No and this is my sister Don't."

And today, 50 years later, surrounded as we are by an overkill of technology, products, information, lifestyles, intoxicants, food, choices…there are so many more things to which a parent has to say No.

How do you do it without setting off a civil war in your home each time that you have to say No?

Well, just like most aspects of parenting, it's a tough call, no doubt. You simply have to find that fine balance, each time you need to say No, to come up with a *decisive, effective* and *palatable* way to do it.

Here are 5 No-No's for when you're saying No:

⚽ Never say "NO, because I say so." This is the 21st century. Your child expects and deserves an explanation. However, do remember to keep it short and age-appropriate. No point going into Quantum Physics when you're saying No to a 12-year-old boy wanting to try to "drive the car only in the compound".

⚽ Avoid adding disparaging remarks. Say No firmly but kindly, with a few valid reasons. Do realize, that for your child you have just erected a 10-foot high wall of frustration. You really don't need to add barbed wire by saying things like: "Only dumb girls go to discos. Why cant you find more sensible friends?" Even worse, is to throw 'clever' lines at children like: "Which part of No don't you understand?"

⚽ Double standards are out. You can't get away with it – your child will catch you out at once. "Don't do as I do, do as I say" is a totally dated line, and it never worked in the first place. For instance, parents who eat erratically, don't bother to exercise, lug around many extra kilos – cannot really say an effective No to their kids' demand for junk food.

⚽ Avoid giving contradictory messages. The child – whether 6 or 16, needs to feel that you know why you're saying No and that you're consistent. Saying No cannot depend on whether you're in a mood to be parently and hyper-responsible on one day, and in a lazy *chalta hai* mood the next day.

🎱 Do not be drawn into a bargaining session. Once you've said your No, avoid negotiations – something that 4-year-olds can try with as much persistence as can a 16 year old. "If you let me buy this dress today, then I promise I'll wear that boring salwar-kameez to that wedding tomorrow" – this kind of deal-making is not a good idea at all, since hence forth, all No's from you will be seen as Negotiable No's.

Here are 5 Dos of saying Don't:

🎱 Do have some alternatives to offer your child once you've said No to something. This isn't 'negotiating' – it is just a way to reduce the frustration. A sweeping, all-encompassing No is very difficult for a child to digest. A No with an alternative is easier to accept. For instance, "No you cannot watch TV during exam days...but we can go out on a small drive if you want a break."

🎱 Child-proof the environment. With young children, it pays to anticipate situations where you may have to say No, and try to distract them before they get to the situation. This involves, first, making your home a child-safe place, so that you're not constantly asking the child to not touch this, not go there, not sit here, etc.

🎱 With older kids too, you can know in advance if your child tends to ask for stuff in a store, or drink too many soft drinks at a party, or set his heart on branded products that you cannot afford. Of course you can't 'distract' him! So here it pays to set down limits in advance: "You can have one Cola at the party and two scoops of ice cream." Or "You can buy this now, but then for Diwali we'll have to buy you something small."

⦿ Do demonstrate to children (without lecturing, of course) that you too, as adults, are faced with many No's. Children tend to think that parents are created to thwart and frustrate them, and once they become adults, they won't have to deny themselves a thing! Let your children see that you too set yourself many No's – which may be frustrating too, but are ultimately for your own good.

Over and above the grind of school life, find out what your children are good at and really enjoy doing. In a world that seems to be all about consumption, try to find what makes your child tick – that can't be got off a shelf. This involves much more than money – it means that you invest time and energy. But it's well worth it.

O for Only Child

The only child does not have to be a lonely child.

The only child is fast becoming the norm for many families. The reasoning behind the decision is usually related to health issues, financial considerations, social-consciousness about overpopulation, time/career pressures, and the urge to give that child undivided attention and the best of available resources. All valid reasoning; and the personal choice or constraint of every couple.

However, the fact remains, that an only child, however loved and well-provided for, is deprived of one of the most important features of his/her emotional landscape: a sibling. Of course, parents compensate for this by involving the child in more activities, planned 'play-dates' with other children, etc. And yet, the absence of a brother or sister is a very specific and undeniable void in the social, mental, and emotional development and make-up of a child.

Emotional and social processes that get sorted and figured out quite naturally when there is more than one child in the family are: sharing of parental love and attention, developing patience, dealing with irrationality/unfairness, caring and responsibility, and other such emotional and socializing issues. In that sense, in families that have two or more children, such 'corners' are rubbed off during the growing years, consciously as well as unconsciously. This prepares children to deal later with the outside adult world of co-operative living, team work, sharing of resources, relationship building, social skills, etc.

Say 'only child' – and people come up with several stereotypical perceptions and images: introvert, spoilt, lonely, etc. But this simply does not have to be true. In fact, so many only children – famous and not-so-famous – have proved all the stereotyped perceptions wrong. They are well-adjusted, caring, responsible, sociable, happy and successful people. Moreover, growing up without immediately available sibling company at all times, they are able to be happy and at ease with themselves when they are alone too. These are people who have had the good fortune of sensitive and well-thought-out parenting.

Of course, it means that parents of an only child have to work that much harder in certain aspects of their child's growth. What is the singular emotional pitfall of bringing up an only child, and how can you side-step it?

Overfocusing: With all parental resources and energies being poured into one child, he/she often gets an extremely unreal picture of his/her place in the 'scheme of things': as being the centre of the universe, so to speak. Many only children grow up thinking of themselves as little emperors and princesses, entitled to unrealistic rights and privileges, not only from their parents, but from the world at large. A child brought up in this atmosphere, sadly, assumes that he/she can control just about everything around them – and adjustment to the realities of the outside world becomes difficult and sometimes traumatic, right from the first day of school.

Parents of an only child would need to, first of all, themselves keep a perspective: your child is part of a teeming universe of other children, humans, plants, creatures and all of nature. Do notice, respect, and enjoy them too – it does not mean that you love and care for your child any less. This kind of awareness in you will foster in your child respect and an appreciation of people and the world outside of himself, helping him to connect better.

The processes of sharing, caring, taking responsibility will then quite naturally fall into place. Your child too will blossom in a more holistic way and develop a happy, all-round personality, secure in the feeling of real abundance rather than scarcity.

p for personality

The forging of a child's personality takes place in the family foundry.

Personality development classes – they're mushrooming everywhere. For little kids, for teenagers, for young adults. Parents look anxiously for the right one, and are happy to shell out good money for them. No doubt, some of them do help, but can one really buy personality facets off the shelf? Moreover, there seems to be a misconception that a 'good personality' is one which is heard and seen. How often parents complain of their child not being able to 'speak in public' or being able to 'appear confident'. This itself is a questionable premise. After all, a good personality is really about substance and not so much about show.

Let's face it, the core of children's personalities are not developed in classes. They are formed from the womb onwards, in the family. And more importantly, and sadly, personalities are often prevented from developing or are *unmade* in this very place, the child's home. Here are just a few prime 'personality preventers' that parents routinely use, without even realizing that they are thwarting growth.

You'll recognize them – from your current parenting experiences, or from your own growing years!

🌐 Friendship policing: Parents are known to over-monitor who their child is playing with. They heavily screen and sift the company that their child keeps, thus preventing him from knowing and interacting with a range of people. 'Unsuitable' friends and classmates are 'edited out' of the child's life, and new ones found – usually they are kids who are as similar to the child as possible in every way – economically, intellectually, age-wise, etc. Ten years later, these same parents seek out the best personality development class that will help their child to become 'all-round leadership material'. Doesn't add up.

🌐 Opinion regulating: Children with half-formed ideas about the intriguing and sometimes bewildering world around them, often voice their opinions. These may be completely inappropriate or incorrect – and they're open to discussion. But parents tend to, especially in a social situation, clamp down hard on this, with a withering: "Don't talk if you don't know" – or something even more sarcastic. Some years later, the same parents are putting down good money on 'public speaking and self-confidence classes'. Doesn't add up.

🌐 Humour prohibition: "It's not funny" parents often say to children – even when some of a child's or our own mistakes/fears/misfortunes can be seen in a lighter light really. We provide clearly demarcated areas of what is and isn't funny, not leaving any scope for a child to be able to view some aspects of life in a broader perspective. Later, we want someone to teach them how to be positive and successful. Doesn't add up.

It's a fine balance of course, between guiding a child and being guided by his or her uniqueness. But once you've learnt to walk this tight-rope, the rewards are huge – in terms of a parent-child relationship fuelled by love, grace and respect. And a child whose unique personality shines through.

p for pets

Pets and kids is a bond that can be mutually rewarding if nurtured well.

"Mummy I want a dog", "When can we get a dog?"

You've heard that before, probably, right from when your child was 4 years old. If not a dog, a cat, or a tortoise or fish…Your child has asked for them repeatedly, and chances are, that if you're not a pet person, you've found ways of delaying, postponing and defusing the subject.

There is little doubt that pets are great for kids. It's a unique bond, one that gives your child great pleasure and a sense of responsibility, respect for other living beings, the experience of trust and non-verbal communication with an animal…the benefits are many. And yet, so many impulsive pet purchases quickly disintegrate into unhappy and stressful situations – emotional and physical – for the family and for the pet too.

The sad truth is that the presence of a neglected and unwanted pet in the family can teach a child that it is quite okay to be insensitive and uncaring – it densensitizes him to suffering. Once the initial enthusiasm and novelty of the pet is over, and the family begins to neglect or mistreat an animal, the message of selfishness is clearly communicated to your child.

When is your child ready for a pet? The answer to that, really, is another question: Are *you* ready for a pet?

For those who've not kept pets before, there are a few points to think of before getting a new creature into your home:

🐾 While a pet is a great 'addition' to your child's world, it is not a toy or a game that is to be brought into the house solely for your child's pleasure and development. It is a creature that has needs – which involve consistent feeding, exercise, play, training, grooming, medical attention and affection or at least attention.

🐾 Your child may be able to take on quite a few of these responsibilities, but finally it is you who will have to take on most of these – especially during exam times, holidays, etc.

🐾 In the case of dogs and cats, do you, your child or any other family member suffer from fur allergies?

🐾 Are you an obsessively tidy and house-proud person? Pets do have their own distinctive odours and can also track in mud, shed fur, etc. And if your child is an animal-lover, it is likely that he or she will not be bothered with these aspects.

🐾 Do you have any friends or family, that will willingly take care of your pet when you go away on holiday?

Once these aspects of pet-rearing are addressed, and you think you're ready to bring in a pet, some dos and donts:

❁ Get a pet that fits in with your lifestyle in terms of space, money and time.

❁ Avoid exotic creatures that need special environments and foods. Even a breed of dog that is not used to our climate is a bad idea.

❁ Small doesn't necessarily mean cute and friendly. Pomeranian dogs, for instance, are cute and toy-like to look at but are notoriously bad-tempered.

❁ Stop your children from petting and interacting with their new pet constantly – all creatures need to be left alone for a while, like any of us.

❁ Avoid severely restricted environments like bird cages – you can provide a certain area of the house for your pet – and restrict its entry into other areas.

The bond that develops between humans and animals is one that has been enjoyed for centuries, now. Remember, it is one that pivots on mutual affection and respect.

p for privacy

Allow your child emotional private space, or else she will build her own fortress.

"How dare they invade my privacy?" a 13-year-old recently raged to a counselor – she had just discovered that her parents had been reading her diary.

Children's privacy, the 'invasion' of it, what constitutes a child's privacy and what is plain secretive/slyness...these are complex issues indeed, in every parent-child relationship. And the rules and parameters change with every growing year, or should one say, every month!

Privacy is not only about physical space – their own room, their own cupboard, etc. Your home could be a small space shared by many people, and yet all the family members can enjoy a certain mental/emotional privacy – each person giving the other 'space'. And in the largest of homes, with each person having their own rooms, bathrooms, computers, tv, etc...there could be a complete lack of and disrespect of privacy.

It is important, when dealing with issues of privacy with your child, to firstly be able to draw a fairly clear line between what respecting his/her privacy involves and what it doesn't.

🌐 Reading diaries, snooping around in cupboards, listening in on phone conversations – they are all an invasion of a child's privacy. Many parents justify it, saying that this is the only way they know what is really going on in their kids' heads. If this is the case, then it means that the relationship is in a fair amount of trouble, and some positive intervention is needed for you and your child to communicate better. Spying is only going to widen the gap.

🌐 Sometimes we compromise our child's privacy without even realizing it. Your child confides in you her feelings, or tells you about some small physical condition that she is embarrassed about. You then share this with one of your friends, maybe even with several. Most children dislike this deeply, and it does mean that their privacy has been compromised. It is a sure way of ensuring that your children confide in you less and less.

🌐 If your child is seeing a counselor, or confides in some other adult that he/she is close to, it is a complete breach of privacy for you and this adult to talk about what exactly the child said. Sometimes the two adults involved need to talk about the issues involved…however, this has to be handled with great sensitivity, so that the details of what the child has spoken are kept confidential.

…And then there are some areas of your interaction that are definitely _not_ a breach of privacy:

❦ Knowing what company they keep – being acquainted with your child's friends – is part of building a good relationship with your child. However, this does not mean that you must have access to every conversation that they have.

❦ Keeping a broad tab on your child's personal hygiene – especially with adolescents – without actually barging in on them, is okay. However, do remember not to bring up and discuss such issues in front of other people.

❦ Asking for an account of how they spend their pocket money is fine too. Pocket money is really a small and 'guided' exposure to the world, and you need to know where it is going.

Whatever age your child is, it is the expressions, the words, the silences, the tone, the touch, the moods – which provide so many clues to his/her personality and current state of mind. Stay tuned in and receptive to all these, and you are sure to remain a connected and yet non-intrusive parent.

p for punishment

Find ways to pull up your children so that they see their mistakes, but are not publicly humiliated.

When our children do something that 'gives cause for complaint' – something that teachers/neighbours/other parents disapprove of – the situation is often a tense or awkward one. It calls for a fine balance on the part of parents. They have to find a way of responding to the situation appropriately, without over-reacting or under-reacting.

However, often we are unable to do this, and adopt either of two rather extreme positions. Some parents go in for the 'court-martial' method. They immediately come down hard on the child, right in front of other people, cross-examine him angrily, give him or her a tongue-lashing, and could even resort to giving the child a few slaps. They then order him to apologize immediately, also providing the text of the apology: "I am a very bad, thoughtless boy, and I should know it is bad to play cricket near glass windows, and I will never do it again"…and other such 'scripts'. In this way, we feel we have made the child see, accept and atone for his mistake, all in one go. More importantly, in this way we feel that we have demonstrated to people that we are right-thinking, fair people, and will not hesitate to punish our own kids instantly and effectively if they are in the wrong. We are actually ourselves so embarrassed at being 'caught out' by our child's behaviour, and we fear that people will judge us as 'bad' or 'irresponsible' parents. So we need to shout even louder at our kids than the situation requires!

Some parents take the other route, that of the cover-up. They instantly and firmly deny the 'charges', come up with justifications on their child's part, or simply dismiss the complaint by saying: "she's only a child after all". They may even take the whole issue to the adult-to-adult level, mounting an elaborate and loud defence campaign to prove that their child is not in the wrong. Here the parent cannot stand criticism of any kind that is aimed at the child, and uses all energies to deflect the charges.

If we have the best interests of our child at heart, neither court-martial nor cover-up options are appropriate parenting. When such a situation arises, it is best to first quietly listen to the person making the complaint. You can call your child out and have him/her listen too. After this, it would be best to say: "I need to speak to my child in private, and I will get back to you on this." Then, in the privacy of your home, you can take up the issue with the child, get to the bottom of the matter, tell your child that his behaviour has really saddened/angered you, and ask him to go apologize or offer to make amends in some way, if it is required.

This is the only way that misbehaviour can be corrected and your child's dignity maintained too. Court-martials or cover-ups are both uncalled for. They are unrealistic and ineffective parenting behaviours, and will not help in building your child's character or emotional strength in any lasting sense.

r for results

Your child's future doesn't have to be signed and sealed on the basis of exam results.

Once board exam results are out, every family with a child in the Xth or XIIth comes to the end of an extremely demanding year of academic life. The results bring parents some surprises, pleasant and unpleasant, as well as confirm some of your readings about your child – his study habits, her abilities, his academic strengths and weaknesses, her aptitudes…

If you look at the year that has gone, or even the last two years, it is quite possible that your relationship with your child has been severely taxed and affected by the pressures of preparing for one of the first educational milestones. You will have been forced to nag, cajole, bribe, threaten and punish your 15 or 16-year-old to focus on studies, work hard, put in certain number of hours of study, concentrate. Also, during this time, your child will have had to, unfortunately, leave behind some of the essentials of growing up: all 'non-productive' pursuits like music, hobbies, sports, even good old day-dreaming will have been virtually banned or suspended.

However good or bad your child's Board result, it is perhaps now time to turn to some neglected areas. It is thus truly a time to a) mend and strengthen some aspects of your relationship with your child, and b) encourage him/her to reconnect with hobbies and pursuits that nourish the soul – in ways that cannot be quantified in any marksheet or any grand total.

These two 'agendas' are bound together, because they are areas in which you can return to the more healthy and holistic role of parent as facilitator rather than as ring-master. This will, quite naturally, help in mending the frayed nerves and tempers of the last one year and healing your parent-child relationship.

How can we go about doing this?

⊛ Firstly, consciously and actively disconnect from the 'Board exam mode'. Undertake *non-goal-oriented* activities with him – listening to music, a ramble on the hill, watching a favourite film/animation movie, letting her experiment on her keyboards without insisting on practise, practise…

⊛ Draw up you own 'marksheet' of 'subjects' on which you would rate your child – which no Board exam ever will. 'Subjects' could include: Caring, Sharing, Sense of Humour, Helpfulness, Curiosity, Talent, Application, Friendliness, Self-confidence, Self-worth…You may or may not choose to show the 'results' of this examination to your child, but it will definitely help you to reconnect with the inner core of your child.

Suspend your and the Board result's 'judgement' of your child as 'lazy', 'careless', 'average', 'poor' 'not meant for science' etc. Introduce her to people from different walks of life who are doing well for themselves and are responsible and happy citizens. This way, the results don't put a full-stop to your child's (and your) aspirations, interests and choices.

At all costs, avoid holding the Board exam result as a 'tool' to taunt your child and 'put him in his place'. This achieves nothing but a bruised and shrivelled spirit. If your child has an obvious weak spot in some area of studies, find constructive ways to help him overcome these so that he will be able to learn from any setbacks and do better next time, without loss of enthusiasm and self-worth.

Each child is precious and unique – something that the education system at times doesn't allow us to take into account. Let us cherish them for what they are and watch them bloom in their own way, at their own pace.

S for Self-Esteem

A child's self-image influences his social behaviour and growth, at all levels.

As parents, some of our duties are well-defined. We know we have to provide physical and mental nutrients to our children: good food, sports, schooling, reading habits, financial security, medical attention, etc. These provide for children's health, comfort, growth, intellectual stimulation and development, and career options in the future.

But there are a whole lot of invisible and intangible essential nutrients that we provide our children too. These are emotional nutrients – in the form of love, trust, faith, confidence, self-esteem, and many more. If one had to single out any one of these as absolutely vital for a child, it would be self-esteem. We could say that self-esteem is the base nutrient – which helps the child absorb and process all other inputs.

Only if children feel good about themselves can they thrive and soar. In fact, misbehaving children are often those lacking in self-esteem. Since they don't have the confidence to belong through positive ways, they try to make their mark or find their place amongst family and friends through bad behaviour. On the other hand, children who do well, are friendly and popular, are usually those who think well of themselves, who like themselves.

What is self-esteem and how do children acquire it? How do we provide it to them?

Self-esteem is the image or picture of ourselves that each of us carries in our minds. This image or picture is constructed through our experiences and is strongly influenced by the messages that others send – most importantly, by the messages that the child's immediate family sends out. The way we interact with children on a daily basis influences the picture that they construct of themselves. We let them know through our language and our actions that they are capable and worthwhile; or we signal that they are worthless, a burden, and ultimately unlovable.

What type of self-image are you helping your children to construct? It would be extremely revealing to keep a small mental or written log, for one full week, of what you say to your children that contributes to their self-image. All negative feedback in one column, all genuine positive feedback in another column.

Many parents believe that they are harsh and tough on their children, and withhold praise, to make their kids 'better people'. Tough love, as it is called, is one thing. But repeatedly telling your kids that they are worthless, irresponsible, careless, ungrateful, lazy...(the list is long!) is simply creating poor self-images.

While children receive messages from many sources, parents have a huge influence on the way children see themselves. In fact, when children are very young their sense of self is linked to their parents. Hence our own self-image and self-esteem hugely influences that of our children. A father was heard telling his son: "You and me are Big Zeros – so we have to work hard, study hard, only then will the world respect us." Is this supposed to be motivational talk? I really don't think so. You can hear this adult's self-dislike and doubt, loud and clear. And it is being passed on to the child. Nothing positive can come from this kind of talk.

Some ways to promote self-esteem in children:

🌐 Recognize and appreciate your children's special, likable qualities.

🌐 Give your children realistic responsibilities that he can carry out successfully.

🌐 Accept imperfection. Let kids know that mistakes are part of learning.

🌐 Encourage children to do things just for the joy it gives them, and not for constant improvement and achievement.

Building self-esteem in your child is an on-going, subtle, and highly essential aspect of parenting. Work hard at it, and it will bring both you and your child lasting emotional rewards.

S for Sex Education

Help your children deal with their sexual curiosity in a healthy and guilt-free way.

The mother of a 12-year-old boy was extremely disturbed. She logged on to her computer, and found that the child had been visiting a pornographic site. Too shaken up to say anything at the time, she told his father, who confronted the child when he returned from school. At first the boy denied it totally, and then asked in a small voice: "How did you come to know?" After that, all hell broke loose, with both parents threatening to tell the whole neighbourhood, to send him off to boarding school, and a whole lot of other threats and warnings.

The atmosphere in the house for the next few days was tense, gloomy, and angry. Neither parent could put the event behind them. The mother completely stopped any physical contact with him, expressing to a close friend that she now felt 'repulsed' as if some 'pervert' had taken the place of her innocent, child-like son in their house. Morning rituals of the mother waking him up with a gentle pat, or the father horsing around with him in friendly boxing or wrestling – were abruptly dropped. On top of this, both parents had begun to make bitter and taunting references to him now being 'old enough' – whenever he asked for any help or showed any hesitation about everyday chores or household responsibilities. Suddenly, the child's world had turned. At this rate, the child could suffer from lifelong guilt and self-disgust about his own sexuality.

This is a difficult situation indeed, for any parent. With the Internet bringing free and easy access to pornography, sadly, many adolescents' first ideas and imaginings about sex are fed by crude pictures and text. The parent simply does not get a chance to introduce the subject as a natural human process that must *always be associated with intimacy, love and caring.* However, even after such a situation has arisen, it is possible to handle it with great sensitivity. In this way, you can a) ensure that your child does not get overly secretive and obsessed with pursuing such explorations b) ensure that your child has a healthy, balanced, age-appropriate idea about the role of sex in human life.

The crossing over from adolescence to young adulthood is such a delicate and complex process. As parents, let us help our children along, building a bridge on which the child can walk, rather than abruptly pushing him on to the other side, or worse, dropping him into a sea of doubt, confusion and rejection.

What do you do in a similar situation?

Never reject the child outright, leaving him or her out in the emotional cold.

🎲 Never make it a taboo topic between your child and you.

🎲 Never threaten to 'tell everyone'.

🎲 Never laugh, scorn or mock the incident.

🎲 Never pretend it's a big joke – 'boys will be boys' – and let it just pass.

🎲 Never explain sex as 'a bodily function' – just like eating or going to the toilet.

🎲 Always remain connected with your child, even if you're finding it difficult to digest the idea that your baby is now suddenly an adolescent.

🎲 Always keep the lines open, even after you've had a quiet talk, so that your child can bring up any future doubts and questions on the subject.

🎲 Always keep the incident private; even if you do share it with a friend or counselor, do not let your child know.

🎲 Always discuss the issue in a serious but easy manner – it is neither a joke nor a huge crisis.

🎲 Always emphasize that sex, intimacy, love and caring are bound together.

Assist your children to blossom into adulthood and not simply blunder their way awkwardly into it.

S for Social Skills

Foster genuine interest in the world around them and watch your children's social skills grow.

"My 11-year-old daughter can get along with anyone from the age of 2 years to 102 years!" – a mother says in a half-surprised and half-proud manner. Indeed it's something to be quite proud of. Obviously this child has what in old-fashioned terms would be called Social Graces. Which does not mean that she knows when to say thank you, sorry and please. It's a much more multi-faceted skill than mere 'good manners'. It signals the fact that this child:

❀ is *at ease* with herself and the world around her.

❀ is *interested* in the lives of other people

❀ has *an inclination* to intersect in even small ways with others

❀ has the *ability* to interact appropriately

In short, this child is Socially Intelligent. How did she

develop these facets of Social Intelligence? Was she simply born with them? A socially well-adjusted child is usually one who has been blessed with parents who have invested in more than just her food, clothing and schooling. Almost every aspect of socially intelligent behaviour can be taught, learnt, practiced and developed further.

By example: The first 'tuition' in social skills comes from the behaviour and attitudes of parents themselves. Children constantly pick up verbal as well as non-verbal clues from their parents' social interactions. Your own genuine, pleasant and non-toxic social behaviour is a great teacher.

Conscious involvement: Call upon your kids to socialize with guests and visitors. It may be something as small as expecting them to sit down and hold a 5 minute conversation with the person while you are busy elsewhere. Also, when you visit people, do bother to talk to any children present in terms beyond the superficial "what's your name which school do you go to" kind of thing. Don't 'make conversation', do genuinely converse with kids.

Tell them about people: Clue your kids in on the people they meet. For instance, if you're going to a wedding, you could tell your kids in advance a little something about who they're going to meet – an old aunt may be a bird-watcher, another guest collects stuff, someone else plans to go on a trek, etc. This way your kids are already primed to relate to people as individuals and not just a mass of people who they have to smile and say hello to.

Acknowledge everyone: As far as possible, a child entering a room full of people, should be encouraged to acknowledge everyone present – it may be a smile, a nod, a handshake, a hello…even to family chauffeurs and house-help.

⊛ A good dose of reality: Don't overshield your kids from some of the harsher realities around them. For instance, take them with you on a hospital visit, if the ill person likes kids or your child in particular. Even if it is a brief moment, encourage your child to make eye contact, hold the patient's hand, tell him or her something interesting that is going on in the outside world – however small.

⊛ Count them in: Expect your kids to be sociable. They don't have to be the 'life of the party' – but even shy kids should be encouraged to be a little sociable in mixed gatherings of young and old. Sometimes we count them out, saying – "He's too shy, he won't talk." or "She's in her own world, don't bother to talk to her," or "These kids are not interested in us Oldies." This reinforces shy or unfriendly behaviour.

Of course, we're not interested in creating over-talkative, socially hyper kids at all. What we're looking for, as in all matters of parenting, is a fine balance. Once you've taught your kids social graces, it's like teaching them to cycle: they'll never forget how to, and they'll always move confidently forwards!

t for thank You

Being grateful and expressing gratitude are key life skills.

"My daughter is so ungrateful; nothing is enough for her, whatever we provide," complains one mother. "My son treats me like an ATM – no need to thank a machine, same way, no need to even ask politely for anything or show any gratitude to us parents," says one father. "My kids just don't know how hard I work to give them all they have," is another remark that is often heard.

Being grateful and expressing gratitude need to be taught to children. However, there is a fine balance between expecting recognition and gratitude for your efforts from your kids, and laying a guilt trip on them. When you talk in terms of the 'sacrifices' you have made; how 'exhausted' you are; how you 'hate your job' but keep doing it for the family; how you have 'slaved in the kitchen' to make their meals – all such statements and attitudes only foster guilt and then counter-resentment in children.

In trying to inculcate in our children some degree of

awareness of the love, time, energy, money that we invest in their upbringing, we need to concentrate on gratitude and not guilt. Otherwise, you could be faced with an irate adolescent or teenager saying that one sentence that hurts so badly: "Well I didn't ask to be born!" Moreover, teaching gratitude is not just about getting them to say 'thank you' every now and then.

How do kids learn to be truly grateful?

✪ When kids see their own parents and other adults in the family expressing (verbally or by their actions) an appreciation of each other's efforts. Too often, in our families, we consider it too 'artificial' to thank each other. However, genuine appreciation can never come out sounding artificial. And it goes a long, long way in demonstrating to your kids that neither parent simply takes the other for granted.

✪ When kids understand what their parents do to earn a living – not as some great drudgery or sacrifice on the part of the parents, but as gainful, hard work, they develop a deeper understanding and awareness of your contribution.

✪ When kids are also appreciated and shown gratitude by their parents and other adults for something that they do, this works to put them in a frame of mind to appreciate people too.

✪ When kids learn that there are other much less fortunate people in the world, it dawns on them that good food, sound health, a secure family – cannot be taken for granted, and are gifts that one must be grateful for.

❀ When kids are not instantly provided everything that they ask for (even when they are very young), they appreciate what they get, and learn not to take parents for granted.

Teaching kids gratitude helps them genuinely enjoy and savour the many gifts – material as well as intangible – that parents and the world has to offer. An ungrateful child is not just an ill-mannered one, but also one whose happiness is extremely temporary and fleeting, dependent on the next good thing that he gets or is done for him. This is the single-most important reason for why our kids must learn to feel and express gratitude.

U for Updating

Parents need to keep updating their role, as their kids grow and mature.

It's not only children who grow. Parents have to keep growing too. Part of the deal of parenting is that you have to keep growing up with your kids. Which means: talking and interacting with your child in ways appropriate to his age, as he grows and matures. For most parents, this happens naturally – our children themselves, as they grow, demand that we stop babying them, and allow them certain freedom, hear their opinions, etc.

However, some parents remain stuck in childhood – in their own kid's babyhood, when the child was completely dependent on them. In spite of all signs that their child is now an adolescent, even a young adult, some parents are unable to 'update' their parenting role. They will continue to closely monitor how much and what their children eat, what opinions they express, and even what they choose to wear. They will insist on baby-talk, when the child wants to have a normal conversation; they will issue instructions like 'go wash your hands' – when the child is excitedly trying to talk about something that happened in school; they will oversimplify answers to complex questions that a child asks; they will read the child's school syllabus, pre-digest it and offer morsels of information to the child, even before the child can encounter it on his own and come up with his own questions, confusions, and possibly mistakes.

This parent has a deep emotional investment in not letting the child grow up. And this emotional investment is not a healthy, nurturing one. It is one based on fear. Such a parent fears losing her identity if the child begins to make sense of its world on its own. Rather than allow the child to grow up and to grow and self-actualize, the parent does everything in her powers to keep the child at the infantile stage, and to herself remain infantile. Here, parenting becomes the ideal excuse to avoid other social and adult relationships and responsibilities too. Such a parent, very likely, will turn the other parent too into a 'child'. How often we hear women saying: "My husband is a big baby, he's my eldest son." In this way, everyone remains under her control, they do not form separate identities, and her authority is never challenged. It may appear like love and duty, but it is a form of smothering. In such a scenario, the child is there to fulfil the parent's needs, and not the other way around.

On the other hand, parents who grow up appropriately along with their kids, read the signals, and pick up clues about how they may need to modify their interaction. For instance, after the age of 8 or 9, you suddenly find that your warm cuddly son now avoids hugging you in public; you know then that you shouldn't force him to. Or a 17-year-old daughter shows some embarrassment if you turn up at her college with her lunch that she forgot at home; the aware parent recognizes that this is not an outright rejection. It is a sign that your child is now in a social zone which does not at the time accommodate/need you. If seen in the proper perspective, such developments do not turn into an emotional crisis in which the mother believes that the love between her and her child is waning or has now become dispensable. Your position as a parent is never dispensable, in that sense. As your kids grow older, even into adulthood, you continue being a parent, a friend, a guide. But in new, more mature ways, giving your child the space and freedom to be his own person.

V for Violence

However young they are, children pick up on even covert interpersonal violence in the home.

"There's so much violence all around us," parents say today. "How do we protect our kids from it?" They are usually talking about violence that comes through to us from the news, from the media, from film and television programmes, and from electronic combat games. We attribute any of our children's violent behaviour, angry outbursts, and other such incidents to the violence that they are being fed by the outside world.

This is overt violence. However, there is a hidden, and more subtle violence generated right within the family. And this has a much more immediate and lasting influence on our kids than anything that they watch on TV.

Adults in a family do commit and communicate a lot of violence. This may not be actual physical violence or out-in-the-open shouting and fighting. It may be something as simple as banging a door unnecessarily hard, muttering under your breath, overtaking someone rashly, honking hard, sneering and mocking at other people…All of it adds up in your child's psyche.

Sometimes even silence is violent: for instance, when one adult in the family withdraws from another in cold white rage. How often people remember such things from their childhood and say: "It was the most frightening part of my growing years. I could have handled it better if they had just openly argued." We may think that as long as children don't actually see or hear anything, they don't know how violently angry you are with your self/spouse/in-laws/boss/ life. But children absorb with all their senses and with many 'micro-senses' too. However young they are, however engrossed they seem in playing or in some other activity, even when they are not in the same room, children pick up on covert inter-personal violence.

When a grandparent undermines a parent's authority in some way, when a child overhears you talking bitterly about another family member, when you wish some colleague ill and talk nastily about him, when you make disparaging remarks about some community…it all generates violent images and deep fear in your child. Our children watch and absorb this every day in many ways. And because they do not know how to process this, it comes out in surprisingly violent forms of social behaviour.

Of course, minor arguments, small irritations, even serious family discussions on possibly unpleasant topics – such things do not necessarily send out violent messages. Household disagreements, problems, discussions, crises – they are all part of family life. It is how much 'heat' we as adults bring to the situation, that brings in the element of covert violence. The tricky part is that this kind of violence is rarely out there for all to see. In some families you may never hear a raised voice, and yet there could be serious violence being perpetrated there. You can be sure that the child in such a family picks up on the unexpressed: unsaid accusations, silent resentments, wordless judging and condemning attitudes.

How does one tackle this? There is no hiding or clever camouflaging and disguising of such violence – so that the children don't see it. It simply has to be addressed by us by our own inner work. If we give it some thought, and watch how we adults choose to interact, address or resolve issues in our day-to-day life, we can clearly detect and diagnose all our own hidden anger and violence. It is imperative that we work on and through such anger, so that we do not make this 'loaded gun' available to our children.

W for Waistlines

Eating disorders are on the rise; parents need to keep a watchful eye.

"I'm not going to school from tomorrow, everyone calls me a fatso," an 11-year-old says. The words used to tease may change over the years – from 'polson' to 'tuntun' to 'jaadi' to 'motu' to 'tubby' to 'sumo' and the like, but the fact remains that a fat child is often picked on and mocked mercilessly right through his or her school years.

While obesity in children has not reached epidemic proportions, as in the West (one estimate says that as much as 18 % of American kids are overweight), we do see an alarming rise in obesity and related disorders in the urban Indian child population.

Contrary to some perceptions that chubby children are cheerful and always clowning around, the fact is that obese kids lack self-esteem and are often socially awkward and maladjusted. They may make up for it with clowning around, overeating and joking about their weight, or being aggressive, but inside almost every fat child is a vulnerable, hurt and unhappy person.

With children leading increasingly sedentary lives even during recreation time – in front of the TV or a computer – and a dramatic rise in the consumption of fast food, the last decade has seen child obesity as a growing urban Indian phenomenon. We are firmly in a world where most commercially available snacks and fast food contribute hugely to obesity. While this trend is unlikely to change in the near future, there is quite a lot that we can do in our homes – changes in lifestyle and food choices that will go a long way in preventing our kids from getting overweight, undernourished and unhappy.

What can we do to reverse this trend? For those who are grossly overweight, with a corresponding family history, perhaps the help of doctors, dieticians and fitness experts is the main recourse. For kids who are marginally overweight, there is so much that we can do at home, by making small but significant changes in eating and other routines.

🌐 Cut down on bakery products – bread, cakes, biscuits, confectionary and the like. Enjoy them once in a while, and look for whole-grain alternatives for everyday snacks.

🌐 Simply say no to aerated drinks. Do not stock them at home, and allow one, at the most, once in a week. Offer alternatives through summer, like chaas, nimbu paani, coconut water, kokum sarbat, and other such choices.

🌐 Take a family walk after dinner; if possible, walk kids to school or part of the way.

⚽ Insist on some outdoor games at least twice a week.

⚽ Encourage kids to sit on the floor when they play board or card games, work at craft, drawing and the like.

⚽ Avoid taunting, joking or teasing as a part of your strategy to get a child to exercise or eat less. It is always counterproductive, and they face enough of it from schoolmates.

⚽ Have small targets, and every time the child passes the milestone, reward him or her with a piece of clothing or some such thing that he can now get into. You will find that weight-loss brings its own best rewards in terms of better self-esteem, better school performance and a happier disposition.

There is another side to the weight-watching issue. Many parents complain that their pre-teen and teen girls refuse to eat properly and are constantly worried about becoming fat. Earlier, 13-year-olds had healthy, huge appetites, and one of their avenues of fun was to go out eating street food, or burgers, or ice creams, or a great mom-cooked meal in a friend's house. Today a lot of them are denying themselves food, even basic nutrition, in the name of dieting.

Eating disorders are rampant and rising amongst urban young girls. To counter this, one simple rule that has got to be in place: however much your daughter protests and claims that she does actually eat enough: you (or any other adult) have to actually see her eating 2 meals everyday, one of which is the staple diet of your household/community, and one of which is preferably breakfast which includes chaas/milk/juice. If she insists on being on some kind of diet, the only thing you could agree on is no-sugar. But as for dumping entire food groups, simply do not agree to it.

One final word: if adults in the household need to lose a few pounds, just go ahead and quietly do it; stop talking about weight, weight loss, calories, and such like around your kids.

W for Winning

Teach children to take both victory and defeat with equal grace.

'Competition, Competing, Competitive' – these words are constantly all around us and our children. In this context, the closing minute of a TV child genius contest, was a very revealing moment. Before the final round, the quiz master quoted Kipling, who referred to victory as well as loss, both, as 'imposters'. A gentle reminder, that indeed, whatever the stakes, it is playing a good game rather than winning and losing that is of importance.

These are not just words, they are a principal to live by, if we are not to turn our children into constantly anxious, unhappy people with low self-esteem.

Once it became clear who the winner, the first runner-up and the second runner-up was, it also became clear how each child and parent handled their victory/loss. The boy who was declared India's Child Genius, had a quiet smile on his face. His parents came up to him, hugged him and shook his hands. Neither he nor his parents were overly jubilant or excited; they wore their victory well. It appeared as if they would not have been totally crestfallen or destroyed if the result had been different.

The boy who came third too, though he had lost in a neck-to-neck competition, smiled cheerfully and accepted his trophy gracefully; his parents looked happy too. It was the boy who came second – the first runner up – who seemed not able to handle the situation at all. Looking crushed and crestfallen, he was unable to muster the courage or poise to look up or to congratulate the winner. More sadly, he seemed unable to, even for a moment, feel any kind of satisfaction at having made it so far ahead in the race. His parents too, rushed on to stage with grim, unsmiling faces, and had to literally prop his chin up and force him to hold up the trophy. For those moments, he did not seem like a child at all, but a grieving adult – and this, in spite of having a trophy in his hand. How ironic. Here was a child who had proved himself, round after round, and yet, all he could now see was the loss, looming large over everything else.

We need to learn and teach our children how to, at all times, keep a perspective on winning and losing. Of course victory is sweet. But loss comes with so many more wonderful lessons: the knowledge that you gave it your best shot; an awareness of the areas in which you can prepare better next time; and finally, the grace to accept that someone else has simply done a better job than you, *at that moment*. Neither victory nor defeat are a reflection of your core abilities, your innate talent, or your self-worth.

This is not just something we just say as words of consolation to the loser. It is a truth that will serve us and our children throughout life. Along with feeding their knowledge base, we simply have to strengthen their emotional core. Or else we risk bringing up a generation of anxiety-ridden people with shaky self-esteem that can be snatched from them with just the ring of a quiz contest buzzer.

y for Yelling

Handling a raging toddler is every parent's nightmare; some strategies are essential.

Many parents of small children are bewildered and exhausted when faced with their child's temper tantrums.

While the child may be sweet and well-behaved in public, it seems as if she reserves her worst behaviour for the mother, when they are alone. At the slightest delay in providing her with what she has asked for, like a toy, or water to drink, she flies into a rage, starts screaming and may even hit and lash out at the mother.

This is one of those infamous 'meltdowns' as they are called. They can really leave a parent completely exhausted and frustrated too.

To deal with these temper tantrums and baby fits, first, rule out any physical problem that may be at the root of this behaviour. Your paediatrician will be able to guide you on this – a few investigations for any specific deficiencies or syndromes that can prompt rages of this sort. Once you've ruled out any of these, you've got your work cut out for you.

There's no one-size-fits-all solution for the temper tantrum. As many parents say, they manage the situation with a 'bag of tricks'. Many parents in this situation have tried everything - including calmly discussing things, time outs, and, pointlessly, even yelling back and threatening. Finally, they arrive at a few 'gambits' for different occasions; and are able to reduce the tantrums.

Parents try a variety of strategies. A whole lot of parents say that they anticipate what may trigger a tantrum and try to redirect their child's attention so as to head off an oncoming fit. Some say that in the beginning stages of a fit but before the child has gotten himself really worked up, you scoop him up on your lap, gently rock him, and acknowledge how he is feeling. He inevitably begins to calm down, and in a matter of minutes is fine.

Both these strategies work most times, but the weakness in this system is that children are quick to see that you're being appeasing and they can refuse to be distracted and have a tantrum anyway. Then what do you do?

Many parents give their screaming child a timeout – scooping him up and putting him in another room (but please, no locking into bathrooms, etc). Many prefer to simply leave the room themselves and thereby not engage with the fit-throwing child at all. That way, it becomes rapidly clear to the child that screaming and whining are the ways she can be sure to *not* get what she wants.

While handling tantrums is one thing, reducing their

occurrence is even more important. Parents are often tempted to completely give in to the tantrum, thereby getting instant calm to prevail, but in a way rewarding the awful behaviour and ensuring that there will be more to come! The other shaky strategy is to battle it out with the child, which may ultimately get her to stop but takes a huge emotional toll of the parent, the child and the entire household.

Either ways, you are being manipulated by your child, and there's no long-term good that's going to come out of that. The bottomline then is to set limits. A tantruming child is testing you to the hilt and so setting limits is something you must urgently do. Setting limits is for her as well as yourself. For instance, you could draw the line at hitting. Once she begins hitting out, it's your cue to leave the room and not interact with her at all.

Simply switch-off on her when she throws a tantrum. Leave the room, or busy yourself with something, and just don't get drawn into interacting with her at all. If your child sees that she's not getting a rise out of you, then she will quieten down. The less importance you attach to your child's tantrums, the fewer you should see.

Don't get into a reward-punishment cycle when it comes to tantrums. By saying "today if you don't throw a tantrum I will give you this" or "today you don't get to go to the park because you had a fit" – you're giving the tantrum too much importance, and treating it like the kid's currency. Simply become 'unavailable' to your child either physically or emotionally when she takes off. And you could see some results. It needs strong nerves!

Z for Zombies

Adolescents aren't 'sleep-walking'; they have a complex inner world.

A common complaint of parents of adolescent children is that their once active and sunny child is now "like a zombie" – sleep-walking through the day, awake till late night, doing nothing much. Nothing the parents say or do seems to have an impact – they have tried it all: cajoling, yelling, punishments, bargains, rewards, bribes, leaving him on his own, nagging and so on. This pattern causes immense stress and anxiety and the parent-child relationship deteriorates rapidly.

This is adolescence at work, no doubt, in its classic form! There is an overall lethargy, and a 'do only what I simply have to' kind of attitude, coupled with an inability/ unwillingness to think beyond the next few hours, really. It is also a time of self-absorption and anxieties, in which academics seems just a huge nuisance and an interruption to the intense inner-world of the adolescent. It is just an unfortunate modern-day fact that key academic demands coincide with this complex emotional-mental-physical phase of our growing children's years.

In relating to your adolescent child, beyond a point, you simply have to disconnect from what you know is your child's potential, and accept what part of it he is currently able to use. Otherwise you end up always measuring him against what you do know is his own best standard, and find him falling short. From this follows the lectures, the pleas, the rewards, punishments, blackmail and the any-which-way attempts to get him to wake up, apply himself better, pace himself well, and all those things that to you make perfect sense, and to him sound like Greek.

Letting go of your cajole-cum-threaten role is not easy. Too many parents fear that if they let off the pressure, their adolescent will sink into a total stupor of inactivity. There are two things to keep in mind: One, what to you seems like idleness, is often only physical idleness. There's lots going on in that head, actually, but your kid is currently not too keen on demonstrating it to you or anyone around. Which is difficult to accept for you, because up until the age of 10, kids are happy to learn, show you that they've learnt, and seek your approval. But now it's a completely new ball-game in adolescent land. You'll just have to have faith that he is learning, growing, thinking, behind that nonchalant and blase front.

Many parents of now successful and happy young people, remember the time when they watched with some dismay and anxiety as their adolescent son or daughter spent seemingly directionless days just sitting around or playing mindless computer games. However, by hindsight, they realize that a personality was forming, absorbing stuff, thinking things out. All the potential was working its way to the surface. It's just that as a parent it is tough to have faith that this in fact is what is going on, when all you can actually see is your son being apparently aimless, unfocused and plain lazy.

A second reason to back off and accept that this is how your adolescent child will function for a while: if you keep up the pressure, not only will your relationship with him or her deteriorate, he will learn to shut you out totally and effectively, the minute you start in on him. You won't even know it – he'll learn to make all the right noises, as if he is listening to you and giving it all a thought, but nothing will enter his mind. That is the ultimate breakdown in communication.

A third reason to back off is so that you can return to enjoying your youngster's company again, in areas not related to school and studies. So many parents at this stage forget what it is to have just fun casual conversations and interactions as well as quiet tender moments with their kid – which are by far more significant than any academic issues in your relationship with your children.

So take a deep breath, count ten, do whatever it takes for you to be able to grin and bear this 'zombie' phase. And have faith that what your child is doing or not doing right now is not any real indicator of the total personality that will emerge.

JAICO PUBLISHING HOUSE
Elevate Your Life. Transform Your World.

ESTABLISHED IN 1946, Jaico Publishing House is home to world-transforming authors such as Sri Sri Paramahansa Yogananda, Osho, The Dalai Lama, Sri Sri Ravi Shankar, Robin Sharma, Deepak Chopra, Jack Canfield, Eknath Easwaran, Devdutt Pattanaik, Khushwant Singh, John Maxwell, Brian Tracy and Stephen Hawking.

Our late founder Mr. Jaman Shah first established Jaico as a book distribution company. Sensing that independence was around the corner, he aptly named his company Jaico ('Jai' means victory in Hindi). In order to service the significant demand for affordable books in a developing nation, Mr. Shah initiated Jaico's own publications. Jaico was India's first publisher of paperback books in the English language.

While self-help, religion and philosophy, mind/body/spirit, and business titles form the cornerstone of our non-fiction list, we publish an exciting range of travel, current affairs, biography, and popular science books as well. Our renewed focus on popular fiction is evident in our new titles by a host of fresh young talent from India and abroad. Jaico's recently established Translations Division translates selected English content into nine regional languages.

Jaico's Higher Education Division (HED) is recognized for its student-friendly textbooks in Business Management and Engineering which are in use countrywide.

In addition to being a publisher and distributor of its own titles, Jaico is a major national distributor of books of leading international and Indian publishers. With its headquarters in Mumbai, Jaico has branches and sales offices in Ahmedabad, Bangalore, Bhopal, Bhubaneswar, Chennai, Delhi, Hyderabad, Kolkata and Lucknow.

SINCE 1946